الاستنباط من البحر العميق

AL- ISTINBĀTU MIN AL BAHRI AL A'MÌQ

DROPS FROM THE DEEP OCEAN

REFLECTIONS ON THE QUR'AN

Aligning the Heart and Mind

with a focus on

▶ Contemporary Renderings
▶ Psychological Explorations
▶ Western Discourses
▶ Lexical Analysis

VOLUME 12

Dr. M. Yunus Kumek

Address to the Islamic Religious Scholars & Philosophers

Cover Photo by Y. Kumek, Alexandria, Egypt, January 12, 2019.

Medina Houseʿ
p u b l i s h i n g

www.medinahouse.org
170 Manhattan Ave, PO Box 63
New York 14215
contact@medinahouse.org

TABLE OF CONTENTS

VOLUME 12

VOLUME 12

Miracles in the Engagements of the Qurān and Hadith

One should remember that miracles in the works and engagements of the Qurān and Hadith-Sunnah are not the wealth or owned by the person, but it is owned by and all due real and true credit is given to the Qurān and Hadith. The Qurān is Kalamullah and from Allah ﷻ. Hadith and Sunnah is from Rasulullah ﷺ. All the hadith and sunnah of Rasulullah are pleased, approved and accepted by Allah ﷻ as mentioned[1]

{النجم/3} وَمَا يَنطِقُ عَنِ الْهَوَى

All the due real, absolute and true credit is to Allah ﷻ and related to the Rasulullah ﷺ as to al-Habib ﷺ by Rasulullah ﷺ.

It is an adage that "I did not make the Qurān or Hadith with my words beautiful but my simple and lowly looking words became beautiful with the Qurān and Hadith."

Any and all miracle renderings in the engagements of the Qurān and Sunnah-Hadith is given to Allah ﷻ and relatedly to the sidq-truthfulness of the message of Rasulullah ﷺ al-Habib ﷺ.

One should remember the repetitive case the word as بِإِذْنِي in the miracles given to Isa as as a reminder in the Qurān as[2] إِذْ قَالَ اللَّهُ يَا عِيسَى ابْنَ مَرْيَمَ اذْكُرْ نِعْمَتِي عَلَيْكَ وَعَلَى وَالِدَتِكَ إِذْ أَيَّدتُّكَ بِرُوحِ الْقُدُسِ تُكَلِّمُ النَّاسَ فِي الْمَهْدِ وَكَهْلاً وَإِذْ عَلَّمْتُكَ الْكِتَابَ وَالْحِكْمَةَ وَالتَّوْرَاةَ وَالإنجِيلَ وَإِذْ تَخْلُقُ مِنَ الطِّينِ كَهَيْئَةِ الطَّيْرِ بِإِذْنِي فَتَنفُخُ فِيهَا فَتَكُونُ طَيْرًا بِإِذْنِي وَتُبْرِىءُ الأَكْمَهَ وَالأَبْرَصَ بِإِذْنِي وَإِذْ تُخْرِجُ الْمَوتَى بِإِذْنِي وَإِذْ كَفَفْتُ بَنِي إِسْرَائِيلَ عَنكَ إِذْ جِئْتَهُمْ بِالْبَيِّنَاتِ فَقَالَ الَّذِينَ كَفَرُواْ مِنْهُمْ إِنْ هَذَا إِلاَّ سِحْرٌ مُّبِينٌ {المائدة/110}

People made shirk and made the mistake of seeing them through Isa (عليه السلام).

Similarly, all the miracles of Rasulullah ﷺ, in the past, today and in the future will continue inshaAllah as the empowerment of Allah ﷻ.

---

1. Nor does he speak from [his own] inclination.
2. [The Day] when Allah will say, "O Jesus, Son of Mary, remember My favor upon you and upon your mother when I supported you with the Pure Spirit and you spoke to the people in the cradle and in maturity; and [remember] when I taught you writing and wisdom and the Torah and the Gospel; and when you designed from clay [what was] like the form of a bird with My permission, then you breathed into it, and it became a bird with My permission; and you healed the blind and the leper with My permission; and when you brought forth the dead with My permission; and when I restrained the Children of Israel from [killing] you when you came to them with clear proofs and those who disbelieved among them said, "This is not but obvious magic."

At another level, if a person who is engaged with the Qurān and Sunnah-Hadith of Rasulullah ﷺ claims any due in the encounters of the writings or any engagement, then they make one of the worse shirks worse than the trinity claims of Christians as emphasized in the above ayahs.

May Allah ﷻ protect us and give us guidance and do not make us lose on the path and struggle of winning and gaining the pleasure of Allah ﷻ as typified by Shaytān, Amìn

اَللّٰهُمَّ لَاتُزِغْ قُلُوْبَنَا بَعْدَ إِذْ هَدَيْتَنَا وَ هَبْلَنَا مِنْ لَدُنْكَ رَحْمَتاً إِنَّكَ أَنْتَ أَلْوَهَّاب

Allahumma La Tuzigh Qulubuna Ba'da iz Hadaytana wa Hablana min ladunka Rahmatan Innaka Antal Wahhab.

اَللّٰهُمَّ لَاتَكِلْنِيْ نَفْسِيْ طَرَفَةَ عَيْن، آمِيْن

Allahumma La takilni nafsi tarfata A'yn, Amìn.

أَللّٰهُمَّ صَلِّ عَلٰى سَيِّدِنَا وَحِبِيْبَنَا مُحَمَّد ﷺ
Allahumma Salli Ala Sayyidina wa Habibina Muhammad ﷺ

Public Entity of the Miracles as Owned by Allah ﷻ in the Qurān and Hadith

Miracles in the works of the Qurān and Hadith are not random coincidences. Everything has a purpose and meaning in life and is a sign from Allah ﷻ. All these signs are miracles that show the authentic position of the Qurān and Sunnah of Rasulullah ﷺ to encourage us and to give us hope especially at the times, Muslims lose much hope. All the Minnah, due Credit is to Allah ﷻ and Rasulullah ﷺ. If we, with our sinful hands, are used as a vehicle, then we get the honor and hope that Allah ﷻ forgive us inshAllah with Divine Mercy and Rahmah. This mentioned as [3] يَمُنُّونَ عَلَيْكَ أَنْ أَسْلَمُوا قُل لَّا تَمُنُّوا عَلَيَّ إِسْلَامَكُم بَلِ اللَّهُ يَمُنُّ عَلَيْكُمْ أَنْ هَدَاكُمْ لِلْإِيمَانِ إِن كُنتُمْ صَادِقِينَ {الحجرات/17}.

---

3. They consider it a favor to you that they have accepted Islam. Say, "Do not consider your Islam a favor to me. Rather, Allah has conferred favor upon you that He has guided you to the faith, if you should be truthful."

Previously, there was a hesitancy to write these miracles. These miracles really happen a lot in the works of the Qurān and Hadith. Yet, Allahu A'lam, it may be useful to mention them to give hope to all of us and make them as a public entity of common benefit owned all by Allah ﷻ and sourced from the Qurān and Sunnah instead of the selfish arrogant renderings of the nafs, claiming them for its own entity or ego, making shirk and kufr.

اللَّهُمَّ لَا تُزِغْ قُلُوبَنَا بَعْدَ إِذْ هَدَيْتَنَا وَهَبْ لَنَا مِن لَّدُنكَ رَحْمَةً إِنَّكَ أَنتَ الْوَهَّابُ آمِيْن

Allahumma La Tuzigh Qulubuna b'ada iz hadaytana wa hablana min ladunka Rahmatan Innaka antal Wahhab. Amìn.

أَللَّهُمَّ صَلِّ عَلَى سَيِّدِنَا وَحبِيْبِنَا مُحَمَّد ﷺ

Allahumma Salli ala Sayyidina wa Habibina Muhammad ﷺ.

Juz 1

Sûrah 1 al-Fātiha

[5][4]

إِيَّاكَ نَعْبُدُ وإِيَّاكَ نَسْتَعِينُ {الفاتحة/5}

Sometimes, we lose our real-identity and go with the flow of people, events, and incidents. This can indeed induce the states of gaflah-heedlessness in the person. The person can require a self-check and balance if he or she is letting oneself in the flow in accordance with the preferences of Allah ﷻ or not.

Sometimes, we want to micro-manage ourselves and the things and people around us. This can induce the states of gaflah-heedlessness in the person. The person can require a self-check and balance if he or she is losing the natural-fitri states of flow of the incidents and events but trying to swim against the flow and losing all one's energy and the primary goal and purpose of pleasing Allah ﷻ on the path of implementing the preferences of Allah ﷻ.

Everything needs balance.

The best way to establish balance is going back to Allah ﷻ and asking for help with dua.

---

4. It is You we worship and You we ask for help.

If the person sincerely turns to Allah ﷻ with إِيَّاكَ نَعْبُدُ وإِيَّاكَ نَسْتَعِينُ
{الفاتحة/5}then, the doors can open for the person with ease and Barakah and the person may be amazed, SubhanAllah!

اَللّهُمَّ يَسِّر وَلا تُعَسِّر وَتَمِّم بِلْخَيْر ، آمِيْن

Allahumma Yassir wa la Tu'assir wa tammim bil-Khayr, Amìn

اَللّهُمَّ صَلِّ عَلى سَيِّدِنَا مُحَمَّد ﷺ أَلْحَبِيْب ﷺ

Allahumma Salli Ala Sayyidina Muhammad ﷺ al-Habìb ﷺ.

Sûrah 2 al-Baqara

[25]⁵

Memories of Food

وَبَشِّر الَّذِين آمَنُواْ وَعَمِلُواْ الصَّالِحَاتِ أَنَّ لَهُمْ جَنَّاتٍ تَجْرِي مِن تَحْتِهَا الأَنْهَارُ كُلَّمَا رُزِقُواْ مِنْهَا مِن ثَمَرَةٍ رِّزْقاً قَالُواْ هَذَا الَّذِي رُزِقْنَا مِن قَبْلُ وَأُتُواْ بِهِ مُتَشَابِهاً وَلَهُمْ فِيهَا أَزْوَاجٌ مُطَهَّرَةٌ وَهُمْ فِيهَا خَالِدُونَ

{البقرة/25}

One should remember that the person has an implied fear for the things that he or she does not know.

Even in the case of food, when a person eats something that he or she does not know the taste of it, then there is an initial fear of eating and adapting that food as a habit of eating.

Most of the time, our habits of eating extend when a specific type is presented then there are different variations of this specific type. Then, slowly, we adapt our tongues and tastes to different variations of the same food over time because we already knew original and unadopted version of that food.

Similarly, Allah ﷻ mentions in the ayah as كُلَّمَا رُزِقُواْ مِنْهَا مِن ثَمَرَةٍ رِّزْقاً. قَالُواْ هَذَا الَّذِي رُزِقْنَا مِن قَبْلُ وَأُتُواْ بِهِ مُتَشَابِهاً. Having a prior experience of good

---

5. And give good tidings to those who believe and do righteous deeds that they will have gardens [in Paradise] beneath which rivers flow. Whenever they are provided with a provision of fruit therefrom, they will say, "This is what we were provided with before." And it is given to them in likeness. And they will have therein purified spouses, and they will abide therein eternally.

memory can make the person build new memories in his or her present time with other engagements of the extension of the same memory.

If this memory is built with a pleasant and joyful experience of a food item, then new good memories can be built with the extensions of the original experience in this life.

In this sense, we don't have the fear of trying something and having a negative experience from it. We already have some affinity with this particular engagement or food in this case, now we want to explore with different varieties, and tastes. Allahu A'lam.

اللَّهُمَّ صَلِّ عَلَى سَيِّدِنَا وَحبيْبَنَا مُحَمَّد ﷺ

Allahumma Salli ala Sayyidina wa Habibina Muhammad ﷺ.

[30-33][6]

Ana & La ilaha illa Allah

وَإِذْ قَالَ رَبُّكَ لِلْمَلَائِكَةِ إِنِّي جَاعِلٌ فِي الأَرْضِ خَلِيفَةً قَالُوا أَتَجْعَلُ فِيهَا مَن يُفْسِدُ فِيهَا وَيَسْفِكُ الدِّمَاء وَنَحْنُ نُسَبِّحُ بِحَمْدِكَ وَنُقَدِّسُ لَكَ قَالَ إِنِّي أَعْلَمُ مَا لاَ تَعْلَمُونَ {البقرة/30} وَعَلَّمَ آدَمَ الأَسْمَاء كُلَّهَا ثُمَّ عَرَضَهُمْ عَلَى الْمَلَائِكَةِ فَقَالَ أَنبِئُونِي بِأَسْمَاء هَؤُلاء إِن كُنتُمْ صَادِقِينَ {البقرة/31} قَالُواْ سُبْحَانَكَ لاَ عِلْمَ لَنَا إِلاَّ مَا عَلَّمْتَنَا إِنَّكَ أَنتَ الْعَلِيمُ الْحَكِيمُ {البقرة/32} قَالَ يَا آدَمُ أَنبِئْهُم بِأَسْمَآئِهِمْ فَلَمَّا أَنبَأَهُمْ بِأَسْمَآئِهِمْ قَالَ أَلَمْ أَقُل لَّكُمْ إِنِّي أَعْلَمُ غَيْبَ السَّمَاوَاتِ وَالأَرْضِ وَأَعْلَمُ مَا تُبْدُونَ وَمَا كُنتُمْ تَكْتُمُونَ

{البقرة/33}

One should remember that one of our main struggles in this life is I'lm of marifatullah. The other is removing the frictions of the nafs in blocking and veiling us to embody La ilaha illa Allah on the path of marifatullah.

---

6. **[2:30]** And [mention, O Muhammad], when your Lord said to the angels, "Indeed, I will make upon the earth a successive authority." They said, "Will You place upon it one who causes corruption therein and sheds blood, while we declare Your praise and sanctify You?" Allah said, "Indeed, I know that which you do not know. **[2:31]** And He taught Adam the names - all of them. Then He showed them to the angels and said, "Inform Me of the names of these, if you are truthful." **[2:32]** They said, "Exalted are You; we have no knowledge except what You have taught us. Indeed, it is You who is the Knowing, the Wise." **[2:33]** He said, "O Adam, inform them of their names." And when he had informed them of their names, He said, "Did I not tell you that I know the unseen [aspects] of the heavens and the earth? And I know what you reveal and what you have concealed."

The word ikhlās or Sûrah ikhlās emphasizes removing ana, the nafs on the path of marifatullah but focusing on La ilaha illa Allah.

The amanah of ana or self is a tool with a free choice and free will to choose to excel on the path of 'ilm in order to reach to the highest levels of marifatullah as mentioned وَعَلَّمَ آدَمَ الأَسْمَاء كُلَّهَا.

On the other hand, the amanah of ana as a self or ego has a perspective that can be opposite to the reality of La ilaha illa Allah.

The ability of decision making, free will and free choice can make the ana or self to assume an identity of deity expecting recognition, expectancy of appreciation, uluhiyyah-kibriya and idolizing oneself.

Yet, since ana-self has wrong assumptions of this self-identity of a deity, then all these related dispositions such as recognition, expectancy of appreciation, uluhiyyah-kibriya, and idolizing oneself becomes a disease for the self or ego. One can call this as the diseases of the heart. These diseases are aggravated by external viruses of Shayātin.

One should remember that La ilaha illa Allah indicates, emphasizes and reminds the person all the pseudo and fake expectations of the self or ana. The reality of all recognition is only for Allah ﷻ referred as imān for the person, only true appreciation is for Allah ﷻ referred as hamd, and Only Uluhiyyah with Kibriya is only but only true for Allah ﷻ referred as tasbìh and takbìr. The combined form all as La ilaha illa Allah, Alhmadulillah, SubhanAllah, and Allahuakbar are called 'ubudiyyah.

If ana claims some of these traits, then it becomes diseased such as riyā-showing off, arrogance, and other diseases as outlined in the literature of the pious salaf.

The position of ana, self or ego is to relate itself with La ilaha illa Allah if it wants a true value, recognition, and expectancy of appreciation.

This relation is called imān. Struggle of this relation against the temptation of ana is called 'ubudiyyah to Allah ﷻ.

Therefore,

- ▶ It is important humble oneself in front of the reality of La ilaha illa Allah.
- ▶ It is important to constantly teach ana about La ilaha illa Allah which constantly claims the opposite in its actions.
- ▶ It is important to diagnose one's diseases of the heart due to the diseased perspective of ana, claiming deity

► It is important to humble oneself with intentional actions and deeds that would humble ana when it always claims its exclusivity, superiority and self-identity as something impeccable.

One can review the practices of pious salaf to be with the people of miskin but not in the gatherings of kings or sultans in order not to justify this natural tendencies of ana or self.

Yes, the matter is so serious but not easy.

One should really feel the pain in their heart as a concern about one's own spiritual diseases of the heart due to the fake claims of ana leading the person to destruction in this life and afterlife.

One should remember that evil-seeming incidents are given to the person with a hikmah-wisdom to destroy with a harsh and painful surgery either stopping the metastasis of ana claiming deity or removing it fully.

Yet, in some of the cases, the ana takes control of the self similar to metastasized cancer in the entire body of the person, and there is only few months left for the patient to live. Then, everyone around this person treats him or her like a king due to his or her few last moments in life.

Similarly, in this case of ana metastasized in all body, Allah ﷻ opens all the doors of luxury livable conditions as an istidraj for the last moments of this unfortunate person who missed a boat of hidayah and all heart and mind became metastasized with the cancer of ana.

We should see ourselves like this patient whose body is metastasized with malignant cells of ana and we have few moments left in this life.

Yet, in all cases of metastasis, when there is no hope as mentioned by the specialists and team of doctors, when the person turns with humbleness, regret, tawbah and crying to the One Who is The Real Cause of all causalities, Allah ﷻ, Allah ﷻ can show anytime miracles to remind and emphasize for us that:

► The Divine Rahmah is always dominant.
► Allah ﷻ can always make possibilities from impossibilities to show us the One Real Only Deity, Uluhiyyah Who is Allah ﷻ.

▶ May Allah ☙ make us not die under the influence of killing cancer of ana destroying our life and afterlife, Amìn.

▶ May Allah ☙ help us in this very difficult task of claims of La ilaha illa Allah but we are doing the opposite with our actions, thoughts and feelings, Amìn.

▶ May Allah ☙ not leave us with our own dangerous self that can kill us quicker and worse than a phantom snake.

▶ May Allah ☙ make us follow the path of the Habib ☙

▶ Allahumma Salli ala Sayyidina Muhammad ☙ al Habìb ☙

Distinction of creation from Allah ☙

One should remember that Allah ☙ is separate than the creation. Al-Khaliq is separate than the makhlûq.

Some of the approaches of pantheism mix these perspectives and claim polytheistic perspectives.

One should remember that Allah ☙ is One and Unique as La ilaha illa Allah indicates and al-Ahad, al-Wāhid, al-Samad all indicate and require this reality.

Yet, creation-makhlûqat are many as created by Allah ☙.

The relationship between Al-Khāliq, the Creator, and al-makhlûq-all the creation is separate and distinct. The relationship between the Creator and creation is called 'ubudiyyah. Everything in their relationship with Allah ☙ has the position of being an a'bd as mentioned[7] إِن كُلُّ مَن فِي السَّمَاوَاتِ وَالْأَرْضِ إِلَّا آتِي الرَّحْمَنِ عَبْدًا {مريم/93}.

To emphasize this point, one can analyze the expression[8] وَعَلَّمَ آدَمَ الْأَسْمَاءَ كُلَّهَا ثُمَّ عَرَضَهُمْ عَلَى الْمَلَائِكَةِ. The word عَرَضَهُمْ can indicate the names and information about beings. The pronoun هُم can indicate the separation and distinctness of these things as beings created by Allah ☙ as creation from Allah ☙ as the Creator ☙.

Naming & Detailing: I'lm & Ubudiyyah

The name آدَم can indicate specificity of Adam (عليه السلام) and all the human beings in his offspring in its general form.

---

7. There is no one in the heavens and earth but that he comes to the Most Merciful as a servant.

8. And He taught Adam the names - all of them. Then He showed them to the angels"

The word الأَسْمَاء can indicate signs of the things being identified with a tag to be separated from others. One should remember that I'lm, knowledge or science develops and advances by naming things. Each naming includes a detailed feature of that thing in their intrinsic and or relational quality with other beings. Even one can remember the detailing of abstract concepts in math or physics for example related with dimensions or quantum physics that all are based on representations and naming with convoluted meanings with Greek letters or symbols with superscripts or lower scripts. These symbols have all meanings for the ones who defined them initially and built on those representations.

Similarly, Allah ﷻ created everything and everything has a representation in their outer form. The person recognizes these beings with some meanings and names them. The person furthers this initial recognition with knowledge with further detailing of this being. This is leads to what we call as "science" or "a discipline in science".

Disciplines of a science are built on:

1.   Identification/Recognition of a being or phenomenon.
2.   Further Data Mining about this being or phenomenon.
3.   Further Analysis and Critical approaches about this being or phenomenon.
4.   Formation of a scientific discipline about this being or phenomenon.

For example, let's take the example of lungs in human body.

1.   Humans recognize the existence of lungs in a body and name them as "lung."
2.   Humans further observe acquire data about lungs
3.   Humans analyze the functions the lungs with different approaches and its relations.

By acquiring data and analysis, they define other terms, for example, pulmonaria, meaning that "a plant of a genus that includes lungwort." Then, they realize an artery related with the lungs and call them pulmonary artery that is "the artery carrying blood from the right ventricle of the heart to the lungs for oxygenation." They observe a vein naming it as the pulmonary vein which is a vein carrying oxygenated blood from the lungs to the left atrium of the heart [1].

Then, humans observe some malfunctioning conditions with lungs as "pulmonary emphysema" which is a condition in which the air sacs of the lungs are damaged and enlarged, causing breathlessness [1]. Then, they discover and relate diseases related with lungs such as a tuberculosis "infectious bacterial disease characterized by the growth of nodules (tubercles) in the tissues, especially the lungs." Or, the recent virus of COVID 19 or Corona Virus directly affecting the function of lungs and being deadly for the person.

1. Then, humans name a specialized branch, scientific and medical discipline and a department as "department of pulmonary" in order to indicate issues, understandings, and diseases related with lungs.

When we analyze the expression ثُمَّ عَرَضَهُمْ, the part عَرَضَهُمْ can indicate the display of different and countless names or sciences as if a person is visiting a showroom looking at the samples.

SubhanAllah,

▶ When we think about the billions or countless creation of Allah ﷻ from medicine, astronomy, geography, physics, chemistry, anatomy, physiology, and other fields, and

▶ When we imagine billions of books written in these fields in libraries, and

▶ When we imagine what we understand, name and form as a discipline is really nothing compared to what we did not as humans in the universe, then

We naturally say SubhanAllah, AllahuAkbar and also utter similar to angels as[9] {البقرة/32} سُبْحَانَكَ لاَ عِلْمَ لَنَا إِلاَّ مَا عَلَّمْتَنَا إِنَّكَ أَنتَ الْعَلِيمُ الْحَكِيمُ

In this regard, the purpose of I'lm really is to humble the person, humans, all creation including the angels in front of Rabbul A'lamìn Who is al-Bakì, al-Hayy, and al-Qayyum. The name of this natural-fitri humbleness and humility in front of Rabbul A'lamin is called ubudiyyah and our position is called being an a'bd of Our Creator, Allah ﷻ, Rabbul A'lamìn.

---

9. They said, "Exalted are You; we have no knowledge except what You have taught us. Indeed, it is You who is the Knowing, the Wise."

This amazement in front of Qudrah and Azamah of Allah ﷻ naturally make us embody the ubudiyyah of Allah ﷻ as the a'bd in front of Our Khāliq, Allah ﷻ.

May Allah ﷻ forgive us and forgive our shortcomings and transform our shortcomings into Khayr with the Divine Karam and Fadl and Grace, Amìn!

May Allah ﷻ do not leave us with our own nafs claiming deity in contrary to La ilaha illa Allah and making zulm-oppression with lies, Amìn!

May Allah ﷻ clean our hearts and minds from absence of Adab with Allah ﷻ and Rasulullah ﷺ and about all the ahlullah ﷺ, Amìn!

May Allah ﷻ make us love the things within the Divine Pleasure and make us dislike the things that Allah ﷻ is displeased, Amìn!

May Allah ﷻ do not make us leave the path of al-Mustafa ﷺ and all other salaf on his ﷺ path, Amìn!

اَللَّهُمَّ صَلِّ عَلَى سَيِّدِنَا مُحَمَّد ﷺ اَلْمُصْطَفَى ﷺ، آمِيْن

Allahumma Salli ala Sayyidina wa Habibina Muhammad ﷺ al-Mustafa ﷺ, Amìn!

When we analyze the above they in the tafāsir of our salaf, there are very interesting points emerge.

As reported in the tafsir of Baghawi (rahimahullah) [2], Ibn Abbas (رضي الله عنه), Mujahid (رحمه الله) and Qatada (رحمه الله) mentioned that the expression وَعَلَّمَ آدَمَ الأَسْمَاء كُلَّهَا can indicate Adam as was taught the names of everything until the End of Day what is and what is not being created by Allah ﷻ.

It is mentioned in the tafsìr of Thalabi (rahimahullah) [3] that everything has a name. According to Imam Qusayhri (رحمه الله) the word لأَسْمَاء indicate the zāhir-external sciences [4]. According to Abu Hāmid al-Ghazāli (rahimahullah) [5] that the knowledge of anbiyā is always above all creation and humans because they are directly taught by Allah ﷻ without any causality as mentioned in the case of Adam as وَعَلَّمَ آدَمَ الأَسْمَاء كُلَّهَا. It is also reported that the word أَسْمَاء included everything on the earth and skies. Or, it was the different names of malāikah-angels. Or, it was the information related about the offspring of Adam (رحمه الله) with their names and lineage referred as shajarah.

[44]

The Seriousness of Representing the Religion

أَتَأْمُرُونَ النَّاسَ بِالْبِرِّ وَتَنسَوْنَ أَنفُسَكُمْ وَأَنتُمْ تَتْلُونَ الْكِتَابَ أَفَلاَ تَعْقِلُونَ

{البقرة/44}[10]

One should remember that we judge what is said according to the level, status and authority of the person. Content is important. Yet, the background and existing situation of the person is also important when giving value or not for the content of a message delivered by a person.

In this regard, as a starting point, regardless of the content, the Qurān needs to be listened and paid attention to by all humans and creation because the Qurān is Kalamullah. The Qurān is from Creator of all universes, galaxies, systems, Rabbul A'lamin. Relatedly, as a starting point, regardless of the content, Rasulullah ﷺ needs to be listened and paid attention to by all humans and creation, because Rasulullah ﷺ is selected and sent to all creation, systems and humans by the Creator of all universes, galaxies, systems, Allah ﷻ. This is mentioned as[11] وَمَا أَرْسَلْنَاكَ إِلَّا رَحْمَةً لِّلْعَالَمِينَ {الأنبياء/107}.

When we think about the lives of the prophets and the life of Rasulullah ﷺ, Rasulullah ﷺ had the protected status at all times in his integrity ﷺ of character of honesty, truthfulness and trustworthiness before and after the prophethood. Al-Amìn was one of his titles ﷺ given by the Meccans before prophethood. This was a preparation of his divine mission chosen by Allah ﷻ later in his life ﷺ as a prophet.

The notion of the sifah-attribute of ismah-being protected by Allah ﷻ for the chosen people like prophets actually developed from the existing real data. It wasn't elevation of their status beyond humans as some of the people even among Muslims try to use in their words in the effort of "humanizing" them with the objection to their ismah-having Divine Protection by Allah ﷻ.

This is unfortunately one extreme-ifrād in the encounters of loss of objectivity while reviewing the real data about them. Ahlu-Kitāb went further in this extremity-ifrād by fully attributing them things that

---

10. Do you order righteousness of the people and forget yourselves while you recite the Scripture? Then will you not reason?

11. And We have not sent you, [O Muhammad], except as a mercy to the worlds.

are fully inappropriate even to pronounce or think. Astagfirullah, May Allah ﷻ protect us.

Similarly, even the people of knowledge and I'lm take heed from the position of prophets. Even though, there is no comparison between the prophets and people of knowledge, yet some people of the knowledge took the position for the urge for the waqar-seriousness in their personal lives due to the books authored and messages or sermons delivered by them.

It is mentioned that Imam Bukhari (رحمه الله) in different occasions avoided even some of the mubāh or halal engagements in order not to give any doubts or stain of thoughts for his work on hadith and others [6]. Imam Abu Hanifah heard about the people's thoughts about him that how he rh was all night praying and he felt that "if people had husnu-zann-good opinion about him as the scholar, then he should try to fulfil this husnu-zan".

In this regard, the people of Allah ﷻ on the path of Rasulullah ﷺ struggling on the path of inviting others to the dīn of Allah ﷻ should be at least remember their position and try to avoid engagements and means of doubts since they are representing the religion.

Today and in the past, one can hear a lot of excuses from all religions Christians, Muslims and others that how religious clergy has been misusing the religion for their own benefits for fame, position and wealth. Yes, this is not a real good reason for them to isolate themselves from religion because the person who has a free-will should seek right guidance until one dies and Allah ﷻ inshAllah opens the door of guidance for him or her. On the other hand, the people who are in the works of religion should do their best in order not to increase the excuses/reasons for others when they represent religion with possible doubts and problems.

May Allah ﷻ protect us, Amīn.

May Allah ﷻ give us ikhlas at all times, and especially at the engagements of religion in inviting others, Amīn.

May Allah ﷻ make us follow the path of Rasulullah at all means and at all times, Amīn

Allahumma Salli Sayyidina wa Habibina Muhammad ﷺ

[117]

The Name and Attribute of Allah ﷻ as al-Badi'u & The Fallacy of Human Social
Constructs

بَدِيعُ السَّمَاوَاتِ وَالأَرْضِ وَإِذَا قَضَى أَمْراً فَإِنَّمَا يَقُولُ لَهُ كُن فَيَكُونُ {البقرة/117}12

One should remember that one of the Names and Attributes of Allah ﷻ
is al-Badi'u. This Name and Attribute of Allah ﷻ is sometimes translated
as the Originator: the Originator, the Starter, the Initiator of everything.

In this regard, when we analyze the ayah بَدِيعُ السَّمَاوَاتِ وَالأَرْضِ وَإِذَا
قَضَى أَمْراً فَإِنَّمَا يَقُولُ لَهُ كُن فَيَكُونُ {البقرة/117}, Allah ﷻ originated the skies and
the earth and everything inside, outside, and whatever is related with it.

Allah ﷻ gave them and us existence from non-existence to existence.

When this is the reality with Name and Attribute of Allah ﷻ as al-
Badi'u, then human constructions of children, equivalency, partnership
and others really gets nullified in its basis of logic.

To emphasize this point, when this Name and Attribute of Allah ﷻ
as al-Badi'u is mentioned in the ayahs, then the ayahs before and after
this mentioning emphasizes the fallacy of human's social constructions
related with Uluhiyyah. Here is an example as13 وَقَالُواْ اتَّخَذَ أللهُ وَلَداً سُبْحَانَهُ بَل
لَهُ مَا فِي السَّمَاوَاتِ وَالأَرْضِ كُلٌّ لَهُ قَانِتُونَ {البقرة/116} بَدِيعُ السَّمَاوَاتِ وَالأَرْضِ وَإِذَا قَضَى
أَمْراً فَإِنَّمَا يَقُولُ لَهُ كُن فَيَكُونُ {البقرة/117}.

One of the fallacies of human social constructions of اتَّخَذَ أللهُ وَلَداً is
due to not properly understanding the Name and Attribute of Allah ﷻ
as al-Badi'u as mentioned بَدِيعُ السَّمَاوَاتِ وَالأَرْضِ وَإِذَا قَضَى أَمْراً فَإِنَّمَا يَقُولُ لَهُ كُن
فَيَكُونُ {البقرة/117}.

Here is another similar example in another ayah as14 بَدِيعُ السَّمَاوَاتِ
وَالأَرْضِ أَنَّى يَكُونُ لَهُ وَلَدٌ وَلَمْ تَكُن لَّهُ صَاحِبَةٌ وَخَلَقَ كُلَّ شَيْءٍ وَهُوَ بِكُلِّ شَيْءٍ عَلِيمٌ
{الأنعام/101}. This ayah underlines as "how can you claim child or
partnership attribution with Allah ﷻ! Don't you see and realize the reality
that Allah ﷻ is the Originator, Initiator, and Starter of everything?"

---

12. Originator of the heavens and the earth. When He decrees a matter, He only says to it, "Be,"
and it is.
13. [2:116] They say, "Allah has taken a son." Exalted is He! Rather, to Him belongs whatever
is in the heavens and the earth. All are devoutly obedient to Him, [2:117] Originator of the
heavens and the earth. When He decrees a matter, He only says to it, "Be," and it is.
14. [He is] Originator of the heavens and the earth. How could He have a son when He does
not have a companion and He created all things? And He is, of all things, Knowing.

Allahumma Salli a'la Sayyidinā wa Habìbina Muhammad wa a'la ā'li Sayyidina Muhammad kama sallayta a'lā Sayyidina Ibrahìm wa a'lā Sayyidinā Ibrahìm Innaka Hamìdun Majìd.

Juz 2

Sûrah 2 al-Baqara

[144 & 150][15]

The Highest Optimization of Time, Place, Context and People in the Sciences of Sabab Nuzul

قَدْ نَرَى تَقَلُّبَ وَجْهِكَ فِي السَّمَاء فَلَنُوَلِّيَنَّكَ قِبْلَةً تَرْضَاهَا فَوَلِّ وَجْهَكَ شَطْرَ الْمَسْجِدِ الْحَرَامِ وَحَيْثُ مَا كُنتُمْ فَوَلُّواْ وُجُوهَكُمْ شَطْرَهُ وَإِنَّ الَّذِينَ أُوتُواْ الْكِتَابَ لَيَعْلَمُونَ أَنَّهُ الْحَقُّ مِن رَّبِّهِمْ وَمَا اللّهُ بِغَافِلٍ عَمَّا يَعْمَلُونَ {البقرة/144}

وَمِنْ حَيْثُ خَرَجْتَ فَوَلِّ وَجْهَكَ شَطْرَ الْمَسْجِدِ الْحَرَامِ وَحَيْثُ مَا كُنتُمْ فَوَلُّواْ وُجُوهَكُمْ شَطْرَهُ لِئَلاَّ يَكُونَ لِلنَّاسِ عَلَيْكُمْ حُجَّةٌ إِلاَّ الَّذِينَ ظَلَمُواْ مِنْهُمْ فَلاَ تَخْشَوْهُمْ وَاخْشَوْنِي وَلأُتِمَّ نِعْمَتِي عَلَيْكُمْ وَلَعَلَّكُمْ تَهْتَدُونَ {البقرة/150}

When we analyze the above ayah, one can find a few hikmahs/ wisdoms besides many.

Rasulullah ﷺ does not implement an action and take an incentive on his own but he ﷺ always acts with the order of Allah ﷻ. This is mentioned as قَدْ نَرَى تَقَلُّبَ وَجْهِكَ فِي السَّمَاء فَلَنُوَلِّيَنَّكَ قِبْلَةً تَرْضَاهَا

Everything in the life and nuzûl of the Qurãn has the highest optimum and best purpose and hikmah-wisdom in its timings of nuzûl, place of nuzûl, person of nuzûl, and context of nuzûl. This uslûb of the Qurãn as a methodology in reality teaches us that we should also adapt the optimization of our own efforts with wisdom, place, timing, people and context. SubhanAllah!

---

15. [2:144] We have certainly seen the turning of your face, [O Muhammad], toward the heaven, and We will surely turn you to a qiblah with which you will be pleased. So turn your face toward al-Masjid al-Haram. And wherever you [believers] are, turn your faces toward it [in prayer]. Indeed, those who have been given the Scripture well know that it is the truth from their Lord. And Allah is not unaware of what they do. [2:150] And from wherever you go out [for prayer], turn your face toward al-Masjid al-Haram. And wherever you [believers] may be, turn your faces toward it in order that the people will not have any argument against you, except for those of them who commit wrong; so fear them not but fear Me. And [it is] so I may complete My favor upon you and that you may be guided.

When we analyze only this ayah, here are a few points that are mentioned in the tafāsir about this ayah:

▶ There was a clear stance of disposition against idols and idol worshipping by not initially adapting Kaba as the direction of qiblah. The initial direction of Kaba was towards Masjid Aqsa to underline that Muslims are the people of tawhid with the people of book, ahlu-kitāb.

▶ The initial adaptation of qiblah as masjid-aqsa made ahlu-kitāb to consider Islām and Rasulullah ﷺ as the prophet of Allah ﷻ and there were ones who became Muslim from them at this period.

▶ In 15 or 16 months, the initial message and purpose was already established. With the change of qiblah after this time, eliminated the increasing negative identity issues of ahlu-Kitāb claiming with humiliation that Muslims adapted "their direction of worship."

▶ As Islām is universal, Kabah represented this universality going all the way to Ibrahim as or Adam as in some of the narrations representing through tawhid. Teachings of Islām is really beyond time but did not start with Rasulullah ﷺ.

▶ One of the critical establishments with the change of direction of qiblah is to teach us that Allah ﷻ is not bound or bind to direction. SubhanAllah! As the soul of Islām is the true tawhid, all the actions and teachings of Islām served to ensure this critical point. SubhanAllah!

Above are only few points that tafāsir have many other points to show this highest optimization of time, place, person, and context in the sciences of sabab nuzûl.

May Allah ﷻ make us to efficiently use our time in this life with wisdom to please Allah ﷻ on the path of Rasulullah ﷺ and we learn and implement from the Qurān and Sunnah of Rasulullah ﷺ, Amìn.

Allahumma Salli ala Sayyidina Muhammad, ﷺ, Amìn.

[165]¹⁶

Corona Virus of Riyā and Digital Platforms

وَمِنَ النَّاسِ مَن يَتَّخِذُ مِن دُونِ اللّهِ أَندَاداً يُحِبُّونَهُمْ كَحُبِّ اللّهِ وَالَّذِينَ آمَنُواْ أَشَدُّ حُبّاً لِّلّهِ وَلَوْ يَرَى الَّذِينَ ظَلَمُواْ إِذْ يَرَوْنَ الْعَذَابَ أَنَّ الْقُوَّةَ لِلّهِ جَمِيعاً وَأَنَّ اللّهَ شَدِيدُ الْعَذَابِ

{البقرة/165}

One should remember that the diseases of the heart are many. As one specializes in each type of the physical diseases, at all times and at our time, the specialization in the diseases of the spiritual heart should update also itself with different diagnostic systems and their research, medicine, vaccinations, laparoscopic and open spiritual surgeries.

Here, open surgery indicates the most painful type of surgery. Laparoscopic surgery is a closed surgery performed without cutting the body compared to the classical open surgeries.

All these surgeries, treatments, medicine and vaccinations have one to one correspondence in the spiritual realm for the diseases of the heart.

Diseases of the heart can kill the person both in this life and afterlife. Physical heart problems can affect kill the person in this life in a bad scenario.

One of the greatest type of the spiritual diseases at all times and at our time is riyā-showing off or ostentation.

Detection of this disease can be very difficult and complicated.

As Rasulullah ﷺ mentions that detecting riyā-showing off is similar to a dark ant in a dark room [7]. Yet, it is symptoms can be similar at all times in its generalizability.

Yet, this virus change constant forms and types similar to virus having a similar RNA structure within a virus group or type.

Riyā is very similar to a virus. A virus is "an infective agent that typically consists of a nucleic acid molecule in a protein coat, is too small to be seen by light microscopy, and is able to multiply only within the living cells of a host," [1].

---

16. And [yet], among the people are those who take other than Allah as equals [to Him]. They love them as they [should] love Allah. But those who believe are stronger in love for Allah. And if only they who have wronged would consider [that] when they see the punishment, [they will be certain] that all power belongs to Allah and that Allah is severe in punishment.

Riyā needs a person to survive. In its reality, it doesn't have any value. It is just the illusionary state of the person covering the Only Self Surviving Absolute Reality of La ilaha illa Allah. Similarly, virus doesn't have any effect unless it enters to a host, a human or an animal.

Riyā is very difficult detect and needs special effort and tools to detect similar to a virus that need light microscopy.

Regardless of its size, riyā can kill and destroy all the person's effort in this life and afterlife similar to the virus which can kill the person.

Riyā can have different types, groups and subcategories. It can change depending on the time, and context.

Virus can have different types, groups and subcategories. For example, Covid19 virus is a specific type of Covid virus that is under this category also named as corona virus. There is a specific vaccination for this virus. There are specific precautionary suggestions for it such as wearing a mask etc.

Within the specific type of Covid viruses, different arrangements in the form of RNA can make different types of the same virus. Yet, the most effective vaccination is different for each type although there can be a general suggested vaccination. For example, one can give pneumonia or tuberculosis vaccination to covid patients as a general vaccination since this group of virus mostly affect the lungs. Yet, these vaccinations may not be fully effective. Therefore, a specific vaccination for this Covid19 virus should be developed.

Similarly, riyā has different types and forms in different changing times and contexts.

One of the destructive cases of riyā is in the fields of religion.

As one remember the hadith of Rasulullah 🕌, the first three people of religion being first thrown in Jahannam due this virus of riyā [8]. May Allah 🕮 protect us, Amìn.

In today's time, if we take a person of religion, either a scholar or anyone doing the work of the dìn, the platforms of delivery of the message can change the subcategory of this riyā virus. These platforms can be digital platforms of online broadcasting, YouTube, Video renderings or recordings, sound recordings, live and recorded sessions and all others.

For example, if a person is watching him or herself after a recording even for editing purposes to deliver a message, this can induce a specific category or type of riya virus imbedded with another root disease of arrogance.

The signs and symptoms of arrogance can be more obvious and easier to detect compared to riyā. One should remember the first three people to be thrown in Jahannam that they had all undetected diseases of riyā killed and destroyed their life in afterlife [8]. May Allah ﷻ protect us, Amìn. One should remember that these three people did not claim any apparent form of arrogance. In their apparent forms, they were the people of religion calling people to the religion.

The people of arrogance have another virus that they don't make the Jannah without removal of this disease, may Allah ﷻ protect us. So, this virus can more clear symptoms than riyā.

If we go back to our example, one can ask what can be some of the signs and reasons of riyā for a person who is editing his or her own recordings for message/delivery purposes?

First of all, each time the person sees oneself on the screen as an image or in a video clip with even a good seeming purpose of da'wah or delivering of the message of religion, there is a very high possibility of liking oneself. As this can be the hikmah of the dua of Rasulullah ﷺ, when one looks at the mirror, the person utters as "Oh Allah! You created me beautiful, please make my character beautiful," [9].

So, liking oneself or seeing oneself as a beautiful creation of Allah ﷻ can be reality. Yet, this feeling should be immediately transformed and annihilated before it becomes a problem. In this sense, the second part of the dua as "please make my character beautiful," can tell the person that one has problems in their spiritual heart although they may look nice externally. Therefore, the person immediately should ask the protection against all the spiritual viruses resulting in bad character.

In the same example, the desire of the person for others to see his or her video or picture or sound recording can indicate riyā imbedded in conceit and self-vanity.

In the same example, after finishing the edit of this recording, the constant self-thoughtful engagements of the person, remembering what a great recording was this piece and thinking in oneself as "alhamdulillah, Allah ﷻ used me to make dawah" can also indicate riyā at a deeper level similar to a dark ant in a dark room [7] or similar to a virus that need light microscopy for detection, may Allah ﷻ protect us, Amìn.

One should remember that detection of the problems, and spiritual viruses, especially riyā is a required effort for every individual for their own ego and nafs before it becomes too late. The case of the three people of Jahannam on the path of religion should always remind us the missed cases of detection of this virus and resulting in deadly destructions in afterlife, May Allah ﷻ protect us, Amìn.

Along with this struggle and realizing the diseases and constant unending possibility of these diseases, should make the person constantly but constantly going back to with dua to Allah ﷻ for help, I'ana and protection. This is not a high level of piety, but this is a needed reality as if one needs air and water to survive. Absence of air and water can kill one's physical body but absence of the dua to Allah ﷻ for 'iana, help and protection can kill a person indefinitely in afterlife, May Allah ﷻ protect us, Amìn.

One should constantly remind oneself that recognition of people in one's achievements and their applauding for this person does not have any value. Therefore, their "likes" or "dislikes" do not have any real value. Only absolute value comes from Allah ﷻ.

Therefore, if one constantly focuses on La ilaha illa Allah, then one can try to struggle only for the absolute value. That is the Like or Dislike of Allah ﷻ. Or, it is also expressed as the Pleasure or Displeasure of Allah ﷻ.

Yes, the root reason of riyā is the absence of full or essence of La ilaha illa Allah. A person expects likes from others other than Allah ﷻ. The person expects recognition, title, applaud, greatness, praise, promotion, encouragement from people or things other than Allah ﷻ.

Yet, it is very difficult to detect.

One should constantly try to do a good deed/amalu-sālih to please Allah ﷻ.

Yet, on the way, the genuine goal or the intention or the essence can be lost. This can be due to

either the person didn't have the sincere intention of pleasing Allah ﷻ in the beginning. This can be the worst.

Or, the person had the real and essential intention in the beginning, then this was lost on the path while he was about to win the game but lost on the path of winning. This ending is definitely the most sad.

May Allah ﷻ protect us from all bad and sad ending, Amìn.

Yet, at all times and at all cases, one should run to Allah ﷻ to ask help, and I'ana to purify one's intention and Allah ﷻ keep him or her in istiqamah on the path. Allahumma Ja'alna minhum, Amìn

The expression as "the person of heart" indicates a person who has the constant struggle of connecting oneself with one's own heart in order to detect these diseases and ask help from Allah ﷻ in purification of the intention with istiqamah. This struggle can be called ikhlā or ihsān in different forms.

The person of the heart always try to connect with his or her emotions and thoughts asking the constant question of "why I am doing what I am doing? Is this engagement, thought, even this emotion is liked or disliked by Allah ﷻ ?"

The person of the heart is always in a self-fight with oneself.

The person of the heart can have two representations. One can be seen as a pious and virtuous of a great-valued person by others.

The other is always fighting with oneself with due to the entering viruses and diseases try to kill the person indefinitely. Some of the diseases caused by viruses are riyā, arrogance, self-vanity, conceit, and greed.

When the person of the heart becomes constantly focused on his or her internal fight, then what people think about him or her becomes nullified and in vain even really funny or tragi-comic.

This person becomes so much lost in his or her own issues of surviving but not dying as a munafiq or kāfir although the people can call him or her as the awliyaullah, qutb, qaws, or elect. When he or she hears those, then he or she smiles at them externally but spits on his or her own ego and nafs for being a potential one of the three people thrown in Jahannam as he or she gained a reputation among people but can have a high chance of being one of the three people as mentioned in the hadith [9]. This is the reality.

May Allah ﷻ protect us, give us istiqmah in guidance, Amìn.

The matter is so serious. We don't have time to waste.

What we are talking is not an illusion, but it is a reality.

We hope that Allah ﷻ forgive us and protect us with the Divine Fadl, Karam and Grace but not due to our action or anything that can pull us to the lowest part of Jahannam with riya, Astagfirullah

We hope that Allah ﷻ forgive us and protect us due to being ummah of Rasulullah ﷺ, Amìn.

Allahumma Agfirlina Bi Hurmati Habibuk al-Mustafa ﷺ, Amìn.

Allahumma Salli ala Sayyidina wa Habibina wa Mawlana wa Imamana Muhammad ﷺ

[213]¹⁷

Promoting Unity & Commonality

كَانَ النَّاسُ أُمَّةً وَاحِدَةً فَبَعَثَ اللهُ النَّبِيِّينَ مُبَشِّرِينَ وَمُنذِرِينَ وَأَنزَلَ مَعَهُمُ الْكِتَابَ بِالْحَقِّ لِيَحْكُمَ بَيْنَ النَّاسِ فِيمَا اخْتَلَفُواْ فِيهِ وَمَا اخْتَلَفَ فِيهِ إِلاَّ الَّذِينَ أُوتُوهُ مِن بَعْدِ مَا جَاءتْهُمُ الْبَيِّنَاتُ بَغْيًا بَيْنَهُمْ فَهَدَى اللهُ الَّذِينَ آمَنُواْ لِمَا اخْتَلَفُواْ فِيهِ مِنَ الْحَقِّ بِإِذْنِهِ وَاللهُ يَهْدِي مَن يَشَاء إِلَى صِرَاطٍ مُّسْتَقِيمٍ

{البقرة/213}

قُلْ يَا أَهْلَ الْكِتَابِ تَعَالَوْاْ إِلَى كَلَمَةٍ سَوَاء بَيْنَنَا وَبَيْنَكُمْ أَلاَّ نَعْبُدَ إِلاَّ اللَّهَ وَلاَ نُشْرِكَ بِهِ شَيْئًا وَلاَ يَتَّخِذَ بَعْضُنَا بَعْضاً أَرْبَابًا مِّن دُونِ اللَّهِ فَإِن تَوَلَّوْاْ فَقُولُواْ اشْهَدُواْ بِأَنَّا مُسْلِمُونَ

{آل عمران/64}¹⁸

One should remember Allah ﷻ is One, Unique, al-Wāhid, al-Ahad. La ilaha illa Allah indicates promotes unity and not promotes multiplicity and conflict in purpose, meaning and goal.

When there is a converging unity in purpose, meaning and goal, then there is a diversity, multiplicity and richness of paths and representations of how to reach this unity in our reality.

In this regard ummatan wāhidan can indicate this unity of humanity promoting convergence in purpose, meaning and goal.

The position of the prophets sent by Allah ﷻ reminded the humans this convergence of unity around La ilaha illa Allah.

The prophets gave glad tidings for the ones who promote this unity with the Pleasure of Allah ﷻ in this life and afterlife happiness, peace and ease follow accordingly.

---

17. Mankind was [of] one religion [before their deviation]; then Allah sent the prophets as bringers of good tidings and warners and sent down with them the Scripture in truth to judge between the people concerning that in which they differed. And none differed over the Scripture except those who were given it - after the clear proofs came to them - out of jealous animosity among themselves. And Allah guided those who believed to the truth concerning that over which they had differed, by His permission. And Allah guides whom He wills to a straight path.

18. Say, "O People of the Scripture, come to a word that is equitable between us and you - that we will not worship except Allah and not associate anything with Him and not take one another as lords instead of Allah." But if they turn away, then say, "Bear witness that we are Muslims [submitting to Him]."

The prophets warned the ones who promote conflict, disunity with the Displeasure of Allah ﷻ in this life and afterlife unfortunate pain, agitation, stress and fear become these evil promotions of conflicts or disunity referred as fasād in terminology.

Yet, when we look at today and in the past and review the history of humans, the conflicts have emerged due to the promotion of group identities.

One should remember that diversity is richness unless we recognize our common grounds.

When we don't recognize our common grounds, goals, purposes, this diversity is viewed and displayed in people's minds and hearts as conflicts, hate, and destruction.

When we analyze the verses of the Qurān, Allah ﷻ reminds us to promote our common grounds depending on the audience.

When we are engaging with the people of book, the unity requires remind all of us and all of them that our Creator is One. When we are promoting our common grounds as mentioned in the ayah, then people can talk about differences.

In our humanly interactions, this unity of having common grounds as a human being should be our attitude of embodiment. The minimum of this that we are all humans which come from the words of being humane, humble, and embody humility.

When we really analyze the Qurān, Sûrah Kāfirûn which points our differences come at the end of the Qurān. This can indicate that we first talk, realize and discover our commonalities that we have unity. Even, this Sûrah Kāfirûn indicates acceptance of ourselves as a human with difference of religious identities and beliefs. One can call this Sûrah in that sense the Sûrah of tolerance.

Juz 3

Sûrah 2 al-Baqara

[255]¹⁹

اللَّهُ لاَ إِلَهَ إِلاَّ هُوَ الْحَيُّ الْقَيُّومُ لاَ تَأْخُذُهُ سِنَةٌ وَلاَ نَوْمٌ لَّهُ مَا فِي السَّمَاوَاتِ وَمَا فِي الأَرْضِ مَن ذَا الَّذِي يَشْفَعُ عِنْدَهُ إِلاَّ بِإِذْنِهِ يَعْلَمُ مَا بَيْنَ أَيْدِيهِمْ وَمَا خَلْفَهُمْ وَلاَ يُحِيطُونَ بِشَيْءٍ مِّنْ عِلْمِهِ إِلاَّ بِمَا شَاء وَسِعَ كُرْسِيُّهُ السَّمَاوَاتِ وَالأَرْضَ وَلاَ يَؤُودُهُ حِفْظُهُمَا وَهُوَ الْعَلِيُّ الْعَظِيمُ

{البقرة/255}

Sleeping as a Human Quality & Different States of Gaflah-Heedlessness

One should remember that the attribute of change, ingratitude, and heedless are the quality of humans. Allah ﷻ as al-Hayy, al-Qayyum, La takhuzu sinatun wa la nawm, and al-Shakûr is beyond the changes like humans, beyond the human heedless affairs and beyond having the affairs of ingratitude like humans.

One should remember that in each engagement of gaflah-heedless, there is the very high possibility of resetting one's spiritual position with Allah ﷻ to the lower states.

For example, sleeping is the physical indication of gaflah. When one disconnects oneself with their surrounding with sleeping and dozing off, one is actually watching movies in the dream state. Yet, the choice of movies is out of his or her control. There is a 3D movie presented to this sleeping person and the person actively takes role in this movie.

At this state of sleeping, one can have choice of the movie in the state of sleeping, if he or she uses her preparation the best before sleeping. This best preparation is making sunnah duas before sleeping, having wudhu, and following the state of azkār in bed as mentioned by Rasulullah ﷺ. Then, the person can have a better movie.

---

19. Allah - there is no deity except Him, the Ever-Living, the Sustainer of [all] existence. Neither drowsiness overtakes Him nor sleep. To Him belongs whatever is in the heavens and whatever is on the earth. Who is it that can intercede with Him except by His permission? He knows what is [presently] before them and what will be after them, and they encompass not a thing of His knowledge except for what He wills. His Kursi extends over the heavens and the earth, and their preservation tires Him not. And He is the Most High, the Most Great.

If the person does not have any of these preparations, the gaflah state of sleeping can be an open field for weird and horror movies disturbing the person and making the person further in heedless states during sleep and even, after one wakes up. In this case, the person's constant evil engagement during the wake states in the day time in reality can make the choice of the dream as an outcome of this engagement. May Allah ﷻ protect us.

One should remember that as humans we are always in gaflah-heedless states during the day and night and while we are awake and sleeping.

Yet, this gaflah-heedless states has levels and quantities.

A person of imān as the ahlullah can minimize these gaflah states with the struggle of embodiment of ihsān.

A person of imān as a sinner-fāsiq can maximize these gaflah states by ignoring the prescribed remedies of Dhikrullah as mentioned in the Qurān and Sunnah and by not avoiding from the actions that are displeasing Allah ﷻ. May Allah ﷻ protect us, Amīn.

A person of kufr as a lost wanderer are already sucked into the swamp of gaflah-heedless that his sleep or wake disposition in the day time or night do not have much difference that he or she is already a toy of Shaytān.

One should remember that Allah ﷻ is al-Hayy, al-Qayyum, La Takhuzu Sinatun wa La Nawm—there is no sleeping or dozing off humanly concepts for Allah ﷻ. This is mentioned as[20] اَللهُ لَا إِلَهَ إِلَّا هُوَ الْحَيُّ الْقَيُّومُ لَا تَأْخُذُهُ سِنَةٌ وَلَا نَوْمٌ ......{البقرة/255}

Yes, sleep for humans is a need to rest and relax as mentioned[21] وَجَعَلْنَا نَوْمَكُمْ سُبَاتًا {النبأ/9}

Yet, the states of increased gaflah can be present in the states of sleep.

Allah ﷻ can transform this natural gaflah position of sleep to a rewarding position if the person of imān follows the guidelines as instructed by Allah ﷻ and Rasulullah ﷺ. For example, a person praying Isha and Fajr in Jama'ah is considered to pray all night [9] (hadith

---

20. Allah—there is no deity except Him, the Ever-Living, the Sustainer of [all] existence. Neither drowsiness overtakes Him nor sleep.
21. And made your sleep [a means for] rest

656#)[22]. A person reading the last verses of Sûrah Baqarah after Isha has a similar disposition. A person getting up in the portion of the night as tahajjud has a similar disposition.

In all states, our struggle is to break the wall of gaflah in our twenty-four engagements of the day. During the day time, physical occupation and business puts us in the gaflah-heedless state. Breaking this wall is through the five times prayer and struggling for the ihsān state. During the night time, physical state of sleep puts us in the gaflah-state. Breaking this wall is through following the guidelines of the Sunnah before sleep such as the duas, Isha prayer in Jam'ah, dua's in the bed, getting up for tahajjud, and fajr and praying in Jam'ah.

One should remember that Rasulullah ﷺ indicates this natural gaflah state of sleep do not apply him ﷺ as a Divine Rahmah and Mercy. He ﷺ mentions even while his body is asleep, his heart is still in Dhikrullah [9].

If we follow the path of Rasulullah ﷺ in our all engagements in the daytime and night time, especially in the natural disposition of gaflah of sleep, inshAllah, Allah ﷻ can make us approximate our states beyond gaflah with ihsān with the Divine Mercy and Rahmah.

There are a lot of awliyaullah that their sleep state is actually again occupation with Dhikrullah. Some meet with Rasulullah ﷺ constantly in that state, some get some guidance and openings for their affairs, and some solve some of the problems and unknown parts of the knowledge and I'lm, SubhanAllah!

---

22. SubhanAllah! It is the miracle of the Qurān and Sunnah-Hadith of Rasulullah ﷺ. After an hour this line was written, we continued our regular hadith readings in Sahih Muslim. SubhanAllah!, this hadith was the next hadith that we did not remember its reference that came as inshAllah a sign from Allah ﷻ that Allah ﷻ accepts our work on our struggle on the path of Allah ﷻ and Rasulullah ﷺ, Amīn. These are not random coincidences. Everything has a purpose and meaning in life and sign from Allah ﷻ. All these signs are miracles show the authentic position of the Qurān and Sunnah of Rasulullah ﷺ to encourage us and to give us hope especially at the times, Muslims lose much hope. All the Minnah, due Credit is to Allah ﷻ and Rasulullah ﷺ. If we our sinful hands are used as a vehicle, then we get the honor and hope that Allah ﷻ forgive us inshAllah with Divine Mercy and Rahmah. This mentioned as يَمُنُّونَ

عَلَيْكَ أَنْ أَسْلَمُوا قُل لَّا تَمُنُّوا عَلَيَّ إِسْلَامَكُم بَلِ اللَّهُ يَمُنُّ عَلَيْكُم أَنْ هَدَاكُمْ لِلْإِيمَانِ إِن كُنتُمْ صَادِقِينَ {الحجرات/71}.

Previously, there was a hesitancy to write these miracles which really happens a lot in the works of the Qurān and Hadith. Yet, Allahu A'lam, it may be useful to mention them to give hope to all of us and make them as a public entity of common benefit owned by Allah ﷻ and sourced from the Qurān and Sunnah instead of the selfish arrogant renderings of the nafs, claiming them for its own entity or ego, making shirk and kufr. Allahumma La Tuzigh Qulubuna b'ada iz hadaytana wa hablana min ladunka Rahmatan Innaka antal Wahhab. Allahumma Salli ala Sayyidina wa Habibina Muhammad ﷺ. Amīn.

So, for this category of elect, the sleep state is not called "sleeping" but it is a tool of communication and guidance beyond human limited physical means or dimension.

May Allah ﷻ help us all times, in the day time and at night time, and do not leave us by ourselves, Amìn.

May Allah ﷻ protect us from our own evils and the evils of others,

May Allah ﷻ clean our hearts and minds and make us follow the fitri states pleasing Allah ﷻ, Amìn

May Allah ﷻ make us follow the path of Rasulullah ﷺ al-Habib ﷺ at all times, Amìn.

اَللّٰهُمَّ صَلِّ على سَيِّدِنَا مُحَمَّد ﷺ الحَبِيْب ﷺ المُصْطَفى ﷺ

Allahumma Salli Ala Sayyidina Muhammad ﷺ al Habib ﷺ al-Mustafa ﷺ.

[257][23]

Anguish of Trials and Tests: Anytime or Every time Being in the Possibility of Darkness

اللّٰه وَلِيُّ الَّذِينَ آمَنُواْ يُخْرِجُهُم مِّنَ الظُّلُمَاتِ إِلَى النُّورِ وَالَّذِينَ كَفَرُواْ أَوْلِيَآؤُهُمُ الطَّاغُوتُ يُخْرِجُونَهُم مِّنَ النُّورِ إِلَى الظُّلُمَاتِ أُوْلَئِكَ أَصْحَابُ النَّارِ هُمْ فِيهَا خَالِدُونَ

{البقرة/257}

One should remember that if Allah ﷻ gives the empowerment to the person, he or she can immediately transform from the darkness, pessimism, hopelessness, and trends of not desiring to live but to die[24] into the light, optimism, desiring to live and die with a fulfilling and satisfying goal and purpose. SubhanAllah!

The first requirement of the Tawajjuh of Allah ﷻ to the person is imãn. In other words, imãn regardless of its quantity and quality is the first step to attract the Pleasure, and Help and Transformation of Allah ﷻ from these depressive states into the states of calmness and tranquility. As mentioned in the hadith of shafa'ah, Rasulullah ﷺ is

---

23. Allah is the ally of those who believe. He brings them out from darkness into the light. And those who disbelieve - their allies are Taghut. They take them out of the light into darkness. Those are the companions of the Fire; they will abide eternally therein.
24. The extreme is committing suicide.

given the permission of saving people from punishment if they had an atom size of imān-La ilaha illa Allah in their hearts [10].

Yes, we are currently in the river of tests and trials. Every minute, every second, and every day comes with its own trials and tests.

Sometimes, we feel at the lowest of the low, feeling complete helpless similar to the descriptions of the people in punishment as mentioned[25]

إِنَّ الْمُنَافِقِينَ فِي الدَّرْكِ الْأَسْفَلِ مِنَ النَّارِ وَلَن تَجِدَ لَهُمْ نَصِيرًا {النساء/145}

May Allah ﷻ protect us, Amīn.

Yet, sometimes we really feel "that is it, we lost!". At any time, and at these times, Allah ﷻ can transform the person of imān from the depths of darkness into the spiritual empowerment and enlightening. In these cases, a person can more appreciate their imān and bounties of imān because he or she already tasted the opposite of imān before, as similar to being in the lowest part of Jahannam as mentioned إِنَّ الْمُنَافِقِينَ فِي الدَّرْكِ الْأَسْفَلِ مِنَ النَّارِ وَلَن تَجِدَ لَهُمْ نَصِيرًا {النساء/145}.

May Allah ﷻ protect us, Amīn.

In one of the hadiths, Rasulullah ﷺ mentions that the person does not taste the real taste of imān unless he or she sees going back to kufr as if similar to the punishment in Jahannam [10].

Our need for Allah ﷻ is obvious, clear and inevitable.

Realizing this need with La ilaha illa Allah and-wa La hawla wa la quwwata illa Billah can transform the person with a little bit effort. These efforts are simple, straightforward and clear.

Istigfār can broke the layers of gaflah-heedlessness which is pulling the person into the depths of gaflah.

One can make sayyidul istighfār with ikhlās as taught us by Rasulullah ﷺ, al-Habīb (salallahu alayhi wasallam) [10] [11] [12] [13] [14].

Memorization, recitation, tafakkur and tadabbur of the Qurān can make the person go vertically, spiritually upwards, with the rope coming from the skies, SubhanAllah!

Reading, tafakkur and tadabbur and application of the hadith and sunnah of Rasulullah ﷺ can bring istiqamah while traveling vertically inshAllah, protecting the person from the harmful winds, meteors and blackholes.

---

25. Indeed, the hypocrites will be in the lowest depths of the Fire - and never will you find for them a helper -

May Allah ﷻ protect us and make us follow the path of the Qurãn and sunnah of Rasulullah ﷺ

May Allah ﷻ do not leave us less than a second with our lowly self, Amìn.

اَللَّهُمَّ صَلِّ على سَيِّدِنَا وَ مَوْلَانَا مُحَمَّد ﷺ

Allahumma Salli ala Sayyidina wa Habìbina wa Mawlana Muhammad ﷺ.

Multiplicities of Kufr & Oneness and Uniqueness of Allah ﷻ with Many Names and Attributes of Allah ﷻ

اللهُ وَلِيُّ الَّذِينَ آمَنُواْ يُخْرِجُهُم مِّنَ الظُّلُمَاتِ إِلَى النُّورِ وَالَّذِينَ كَفَرُواْ أَوْلِيَآؤُهُمُ الطَّاغُوتُ يُخْرِجُونَهُم مِّنَ النُّورِ إِلَى الظُّلُمَاتِ أُوْلَئِكَ أَصْحَابُ النَّارِ هُمْ فِيهَا خَالِدُونَ {البقرة/257}[26]

يَدْعُو مِن دُونِ اللهِ مَا لَا يَضُرُّهُ وَمَا لَا يَنفَعُهُ ذَلِكَ هُوَ الضَّلَالُ الْبَعِيدُ {الحج/12}[27] يَدْعُو لَمَن ضَرُّهُ أَقْرَبُ مِن نَّفْعِهِ لَبِئْسَ الْمَوْلَى وَلَبِئْسَ الْعَشِيرُ

{الحج/13}[28]

One should remember that Allah ﷻ is al-Rahmãn and al-Rahìm. Our hearts are in a constant state of search of fulfilment. The real fulfilment is with Allah ﷻ. Yet, our hearts can sometimes turn around to replace this real fulfilment with some covers. Since they are only covers and they don't have any essence or gist, there are always frustrations when the person attach oneself to these covers.

One can think about the word kufr as being the multitudes of covers as mentioned وَالَّذِينَ كَفَرُواْ أَوْلِيَآؤُهُمُ الطَّاغُوتُ يُخْرِجُونَهُم مِّنَ النُّورِ إِلَى الظُّلُمَاتِ

In that sense, the person may be attracted to these multitudes of covers taking the spiritual frustrations of darkness.

One should remember that the person can connect to Allah ﷻ the Unique, al-Ahad and al-Wahid, the One, with the multitudes of

---

26. Allah is the ally of those who believe. He brings them out from darknesses into the light. And those who disbelieve—their allies are Taghut. They take them out of the light into darknesses. Those are the companions of the Fire; they will abide eternally therein
27. He invokes instead of Allah that which neither harms him nor benefits him. That is what is the extreme error.
28. He invokes one whose harm is closer than his benefit - how wretched the protector and how wretched the associate.

Names and Attributes of Allah ﷻ reflected in creation, in events, and in incidents.

Yet, when the person misjudges, miscalculates, and doesn't realize the Real Real, Allah ﷻ as the Unique, al-Ahad and al-Wahid, the One, then he or she goes behind these covers expecting an essence of help, benefit and protection from harm. The Qurān mentions this reality as يَدْعُو مِن دُونِ اللَّهِ مَا لَا يَضُرُّهُ وَمَا لَا يَنفَعُهُ ذَلِكَ هُوَ الضَّلَالُ الْبَعِيدُ {الحج/12} يَدْعُو لَمَن ضَرُّهُ أَقْرَبُ مِن نَّفْعِهِ لَبِئْسَ الْمَوْلَى وَلَبِئْسَ الْعَشِيرُ {الحج/13}.

This choice of the person taking these covers as benefactor, friend or protector what a bad and disasterous choice as mentioned لَبِئْسَ الْمَوْلَى وَلَبِئْسَ الْعَشِيرُ {الحج/13}.

May Allah ﷻ protect us falling in the traps of shirk, and kufr of running behind the covers but not attaching ourselves to the One, Allah ﷻ, al-Ahad & al-Wāhid, Amìn.

اللَّهُمَّ صَلِّ على سَيِّدِنَا مُحَمَّد ﷺ

Allahumma Salli ala Sayyidina Muhammad ﷺ

[286]29

Overwhelming Pains of Life

لاَ يُكَلِّفُ اللهُ نَفْسًا إِلاَّ وُسْعَهَا لَهَا مَا كَسَبَتْ وَعَلَيْهَا مَا اكْتَسَبَتْ رَبَّنَا لاَ تُؤَاخِذْنَا إِن نَّسِينَا أَوْ أَخْطَأْنَا رَبَّنَا وَلاَ تَحْمِلْ عَلَيْنَا إِصْرًا كَمَا حَمَلْتَهُ عَلَى الَّذِينَ مِن قَبْلِنَا رَبَّنَا وَلاَ تُحَمِّلْنَا مَا لاَ طَاقَةَ لَنَا بِهِ وَاعْفُ عَنَّا وَاغْفِرْ لَنَا وَارْحَمْنَا أَنتَ مَوْلاَنَا فَانصُرْنَا عَلَى الْقَوْمِ الْكَافِرِينَ

{Baqarah/286}

One should remember that Allah ﷻ is Just, Al-Adl. Allah ﷻ does not give the person what he or she cannot handle as mentioned لاَ يُكَلِّفُ اللهُ نَفْسًا إِلاَّ وُسْعَهَا.

Sometimes, we feel overwhelmed, helpless and we are at the dead end but there is no point of exit.

---

29. Allah does not charge a soul except [with that within] its capacity. It will have [the consequence of] what [good] it has gained, and it will bear [the consequence of] what [evil] it has earned. "Our Lord, do not impose blame upon us if we have forgotten or erred. Our Lord, and lay not upon us a burden like that which You laid upon those before us. Our Lord, and burden us not with that which we have no ability to bear. And pardon us; and forgive us; and have mercy upon us. You are our protector, so give us victory over the disbelieving people."

This can be at the encounters of a pain due to sickness that the person really may feel debilitated and drained.

This can be at the encounters of overwhelming responsibilities of work, school and house. The work that the person may face can make the person really overwhelmed with different types of responsibilities.

This can be at the encounters of an old age that the person feels these weakening parts in his or her body, memory, and abilities with increasing dependability on others. The feeling of being dependent on others except Allah ﷻ can also put the person in different forms of painful states, May Allah ﷻ protect us.

Yet, one should remember that Allah ﷻ can make anything possible if the person knows how to turn to Allah ﷻ at all times.

One can remember the case of Ibrahim (عليه السلام) and Zakariya (عليه السلام) their wives giving birth at an old age against the norms as a miracle from Allah ﷻ. Beyond the means and reasons, Allah ﷻ can make the impossible things possible.

One can remember a small army with Dawûd (عليه السلام) winning against the people with superiority strength.

In all these cases and many more, there is always an exit if one always turns to Allah ﷻ regularly with humbleness and humility-faqr and ajz.

Therefore, at all the times with all the means, when and where we feel overwhelmed we should again turn to Allah ﷻ but not give up.

رَبِّ يَسِّر وَلاَ تُعَسِّر وَتمم بِلخَيْر، آمِين

Rabbi Yassir Wa La Tu'assir Wa Tammim Bilkhayr, Amìn.

أَللَّهُمَّ صَلِّ على سَيِّدِنَا مُحَمَّد ﷺ

Allahumma Salli Ala Sayyidina wa Habìbina Muhammad ﷺ

Sûrah 3 Ãl-'Imrãn

[21][30]

Common Goal for Humanity: Social Justice

إِنَّ الَّذِينَ يَكْفُرُونَ بِآيَاتِ اللّهِ وَيَقْتُلُونَ النَّبِيِّينَ بِغَيْرِ حَقٍّ وَيَقْتُلُونَ الَّذِينَ يَأْمُرُونَ بِالْقِسْطِ مِنَ النَّاسِ فَبَشِّرْهُم بِعَذَابٍ أَلِيمٍ

{آل عمران/21}

---

30. Those who disbelieve in the signs of Allah and kill the prophets without right and kill those who order justice from among the people - give them tidings of a painful punishment.

It is interesting to note in this ayah that Allah ﷾ mentions وَيَقْتُلُونَ الَّذِينَ يَأْمُرُونَ بِالْقِسْطِ مِنَ النَّاسِ. As we live in a globalized world, people are aware of injustices globally then before.

In this regard, a human who did not lose his or her humanity is expected to disagree with injustices. In this sense, we hear and witness a lot of people in different parts of the world who stood up against the injustices.

Our near history of hundred years can include a lot of names, known or unknown, public or not who were killed due to their stance against injustices.

SubhanAllah, this is again a common quality that humans can find the same grounds to unite.

Today, we find people with different backgrounds uniting on this common theme of social justice.

The ayah can allude also one of the visions and mission of the prophets to bring social justice and remind people the ethical behavior and action with imān, tawhid-Oneness and Uniqueness of Allah ﷾ Who is All-Powerful al-Qādir.

Lastly, the style of the Qurān with فَبَشِّرْهُم can indicate a really wake-up call for the ones who adapt oppression as a trait and legalizing and normalizing injustices at the level of self-nafs with kufr-shirk and at the level of social engagement by promoting social injustices in societies.

May Allah ﷾ protect us oppressing our own selves and others with injustices-dhulm, Amīn.

اَللَّهُمَّ صَلِّ على سَيِّدِنَا وَ حَبِيبِنَا مُحَمَّد ﷺ

Allahumma Salli A'la Sayyidina wa Habibina Muhammad ﷺ

[31]³¹

Natural Love for Allah ﷾ & Representation of this Love

قُلْ إِن كُنتُمْ تُحِبُّونَ اللَّهَ فَاتَّبِعُونِي يُحْبِبْكُمُ اللَّهُ وَيَغْفِرْ لَكُمْ ذُنُوبَكُمْ وَاللَّهُ غَفُورٌ رَّحِيمٌ

{آل عمران/31}

---

31. Say, [O Muhammad], "If you should love Allah, then follow me, [so] Allah will love you and forgive you your sins. And Allah is Forgiving and Merciful."

One should remember when we observe universe, there are a lot of signs and ayahs that we get amazed and say SubhanAllah! Each amazement, ayahs, and signs that we see, hear and feel make us connect to the Maker, Designer, Originator of all Who is Allah ﷻ. Each Name and Attribute of Allah ﷻ reflected in the universe, on us, and in different fields of natural and social sciences make us love Allah ﷻ.

In that sense, there is a natural love in us to love Allah ﷻ if we are not fully blurred and if our senses are not fully blurred, and if our sensational motors are not fully covered as the word kāfir can indicate.

On the other hand, Allah ﷻ mentions in the Qurãn, if you have this natural love and claim of love for Allah ﷻ, then the measure and representation of this love is with the love for Rasulullah ﷺ. Loving Rasulullah ﷺ indicates following the sunnah of Rasulullah ﷺ. In another words, Allah ﷻ mentions as if "if you claim to love Me, then the check point of this your love for My Messenger, Rasulullah ﷺ who teaches you what I am pleased with." Allahu A'lam.

اَللّٰهُمَّ جَعَلْنَا مَن يُحِبُّكَ وَاتَّبِعُ سَبِيْلِ رَسُوْلِكَ ﷺ، آمِيْن

Allahumma Ja'alna man yuhibbuka wa attibu' sabili Rasuluk ﷺ, Amín.

اَللّٰهُمَّ صَلِّ عَلَى سَيِّدِنَا وَ حَبِيْبَنَا مُحَمَّد ﷺ المُصطَفى ﷺ

Allahumma Salli A'la Sayyidina Habíbina Muhammad ﷺ al-Mustafa ﷺ.

Categorization of the Sunnah of Rasulullah ﷺ and Our Attitudes towards the Sunnah of Rasulullah ﷺ

One should remember the source of sunnah of Rasulullah ﷺ is three. One is his ﷺ blessed statements. The other is his blessed ﷺ actions. The last one is his blessed dispositions in different times, contexts, conditions, and situations ﷺ.

One should remember that it is required to follow Rasulullah ﷺ in the matters of farz and wãjib. The negligence of them can deem accountability, punishment and penalty.

One should remember that it is the responsibility of people of imãn to follow the nawãfil part of the sunnah of Rasulullah ﷺ outside the farz and wãjib. It may not deem punishment or penalty, yet there is a great benefit in this world and reward from Allah ﷻ in following this nawãfil part of the sunnah of Rasulullah ﷺ.

One should remember that there are blessed habits of Rasulullah ﷺ. There is a wordily great benefit to follow these blessed habits of sunnah of Rasulullah ﷺ. If a person does it with the intention of following the sunnah of Rasulullah ﷺ, then this simple habit of the person can become an 'ibadah and the person can receive reward from Allah ﷻ.

One should remember that the person who is lazy in following any sunnah of Rasulullah ﷺ will be for sure in a great loss in barakah and in results in this life and afterlife.

One should remember that the person who does not give importance to the sunnah of Rasulullah ﷺ will commit a great crime in his engagements of this life and afterlife.

One should remember that the person who denies, criticize, and does not accept the sunnah of Rasulullah ﷺ will be in great dalālah-misguidance in this life and devastation in afterlife.

May Allah ﷻ protect us from not following the sunnah of Rasulullah ﷺ, Amìn.

May Allah ﷻ give us the adab of following the sunnah of Rasulullah ﷺ in all its minute and major details.

May Allah ﷻ give us in our hearts the true love of Allah ﷻ by following the sunnah of Rasulullah ﷺ and make us show our true love accordingly, Amìn.

أللهُمَّ صَلِّ وبَارِك على سَيِّدَنا وحَبِيْبَنَا مُحَمَّد المُصطفى وعلى آله وصحبه كَمَا صَلَّيْتَ
على سَيِّدنا إبراهيم وعلى آل سيدنا إبراهيم إنك حميد مجيد

Allahumma Salli wa Barik a'la Sayyidina Wa Habìbìnā Muhammad al Mustafa wa a'la alihi wa sahbihi kama sallayta a'la Sayyidina Ibrāhim wa a'la āli Sayidina Ibrāhim Innaka Hamìdun Majìd

[38-40][32]

Dua: Embodiment of Absence of Causalities

هُنَالِكَ دَعَا زَكَرِيَّا رَبَّهُ قَالَ رَبِّ هَبْ لِي مِن لَّدُنْكَ ذُرِّيَّةً طَيِّبَةً إِنَّكَ سَمِيعُ الدُّعَاء {آل عمران/38}[33] فَنَادَتْهُ الْمَلَائِكَةُ وَهُوَ قَائِمٌ يُصَلِّي فِي الْمِحْرَابِ أَنَّ اللَّهَ يُبَشِّرُكَ بِيَحْيَى مُصَدِّقًا بِكَلِمَةٍ مِّنَ اللَّهِ وَسَيِّدًا وَحَصُورًا وَنَبِيًّا مِّنَ الصَّالِحِينَ {آل عمران/39} قَالَ رَبِّ أَنَّىَ يَكُونُ لِي غُلَامٌ وَقَدْ بَلَغَنِيَ الْكِبَرُ وَامْرَأَتِي عَاقِرٌ قَالَ كَذَلِكَ اللَّهُ يَفْعَلُ مَا يَشَاء

{آل عمران/40}[34]

When we compare the two ayahs

هُنَالِكَ دَعَا زَكَرِيَّا رَبَّهُ قَالَ رَبِّ هَبْ لِي مِن لَّدُنْكَ ذُرِّيَّةً طَيِّبَةً إِنَّكَ سَمِيعُ الدُّعَاء

{آل عمران/83} and

قَالَ رَبِّ أَنَّىَ يَكُونُ لِي غُلَامٌ وَقَدْ بَلَغَنِيَ الْكِبَرُ وَامْرَأَتِي عَاقِرٌ قَالَ كَذَلِكَ اللَّهُ يَفْعَلُ مَا يَشَاء

{آل عمران/40}

One can realize an interesting point.

When a person makes dua to Allah ﷻ, the person is expected to put all the reasons, causalities, even sunnatullah as what we call today natural and social sciences behind, and ask Allah ﷻ his or her needs, goal and vision. In this regard, this ayah is the embodiment of this disposition as mentioned هُنَالِكَ دَعَا زَكَرِيَّا رَبَّهُ قَالَ رَبِّ هَبْ لِي مِن لَّدُنْكَ ذُرِّيَّةً طَيِّبَةً إِنَّكَ سَمِيعُ الدُّعَاء {آل عمران/83}. Zakarriya as asks a child from Allah ﷻ beyond the sunnatullah requirements of human bodies in an extremely old age. This dua is a vision of Zakariyya as for the mission of nubuwwah to continue in his offspring.

---

32. **[3:38]** At that, Zechariah called upon his Lord, saying, "My Lord, grant me from Yourself a good offspring. Indeed, You are the Hearer of supplication." **[3:39]** So the angels called him while he was standing in prayer in the chamber, "Indeed, Allah gives you good tidings of John, confirming a word from Allah and [who will be] honorable, abstaining [from women], and a prophet from among the righteous." **[3:40]** He said, "My Lord, how will I have a boy when I have reached old age and my wife is barren?" The angel said, "Such is Allah; He does what He wills."

33. At that, Zechariah called upon his Lord, saying, "My Lord, grant me from Yourself a good offspring. Indeed, You are the Hearer of supplication."

34. He said, "My Lord, how will I have a boy when I have reached old age and my wife is barren?" The angel said, "Such is Allah; He does what He wills."

The real embodiment of dua requires to submit oneself fully to the One Who is beyond the human causalities with the full belief, trust and reliance that Allah ﷻ can do anything at anytime.

After this mode of dua beyond the causalities, when Zakariyya (عليه السلام)witnesses the acceptance of this dua in the human realities of causalities, then in human realities and states of sunnatullah one can normalize the exclamation of Zakarriya (عليه السلام)

قَالَ رَبِّ أَنَّىَ يَكُونُ لِي غُلَامٌ وَقَدْ بَلَغَنِيَ الْكِبَرُ وَامْرَأَتِي عَاقِرٌ قَالَ كَذَلِكَ اللهُ يَفْعَلُ مَا يَشَاء {آل عمران/40}

In this regard, first statement teaches us the needed embodiment of full submission to Allah ﷻ in the state of dua not considering any partnership with reasons or causalities called as shirk as mentioned هُنَالِكَ.

دَعَا زَكَرِيَّا رَبَّهُ قَالَ رَبِّ هَبْ لِي مِن لَّدُنْكَ ذُرِّيَّةً طَيِّبَةً إِنَّكَ سَمِيعُ الدُّعَاء {آل عمران/38}

The second statement of Zakarriya as reminds our human realities of causalities as mentioned with قَالَ رَبِّ أَنَّىَ يَكُونُ لِي غُلَامٌ وَقَدْ بَلَغَنِيَ الْكِبَرُ وَامْرَأَتِي عَاقِرٌ قَالَ كَذَلِكَ اللهُ يَفْعَلُ مَا يَشَاء {آل عمران/40}

Yes, we live in causalties, but we can always go beyond causalties with dua, connecting ourselves to the One Who is beyond causalities, Musabbabul Asbāb, the Cause of all causalities.

May Allah ﷻ make us embody the real dua by going beyond the causalities and attaching ourselves the One beyond all causalities, Amìn.

May Allah ﷻ make us adapt the habit of dua constantly that we find ourselves mostly devastated with reasons, and causalities.

أَللهُمَّ صَلِّ على سَيِّدِنا مُحَمَّد ، سَيِّدَنَا زَكَرِيَّا و سَيِّدَنَا يحيي وَ سَيِّدَناعِيْسى و سَيِّدَنَا مُوسى، آمِين

Allahumma Salli ala' Sayyidina Muhammad, Sayyidina Zakariyyā wa Sayyidina Yahya wa Sayydina I'sā wa Sayyidina Mûsa, Amìn.

[89]³⁵

Suffering and Turning to Allah ﷻ

{إِلاَّ الَّذِينَ تَابُواْ مِن بَعْدِ ذَلِكَ وَأَصْلَحُواْ فَإِنَّ اللهَ غَفُورٌ رَّحِيمٌ {آل عمران/89}

---

35. Except for those who repent after that and correct themselves. For indeed, Allah is Forgiving and Merciful.

One should remember that Allah ﷻ al-Gafûr and al-Rahìm. The combination of two Names and Attributes of Allah as غَفُورٌ رَّحِيم repeated many times in the Qurān as mentioned:[36]

وَلِلَّهِ مَا فِي السَّمَاوَاتِ وَمَا فِي الْأَرْضِ يَغْفِرُ لِمَن يَشَاء وَيُعَذِّبُ مَن يَشَاء وَاللَّهُ غَفُورٌ رَّحِيمٌ

آل عمران/129

دَرَجَاتٍ مِّنْهُ وَمَغْفِرَةً وَرَحْمَةً وَكَانَ اللّهُ غَفُورًا رَّحِيمًا

{النساء/96}[37]

There are many other places in the Qurān that these two of Names and Attributes of Allah ﷻ come together.

Although the person does not deserve, Allah ﷻ sends the blessings constantly.

In our short and limited lifetime, we often forget our purpose and goal and engage ourselves with things that may distract us from our purpose and leave inside us the remnants of grief and worry.

These remnants are normal. It is the waste product due to the problematic affiliation of one's heart and mind to the temporal things in life.

Then, we get spiritual and bodily headaches of suffering due to our wrong choice of using our free will.

Then, we suffer.

Yet, each suffering is a means to turn to Allah ﷻ to ask an exit-makhraj, relief and ease. Suffering is a reminder for our temporality and need for the One Who is not temporal but Permanent Who is Allah ﷻ.

In the perspectives of causalities, suffering is a result of our wrong choice of using our free-will.

Yet, if the person does not want to die under the heavy guilt of their wrong choice in the world of causalities, then he or she should use this suffering as a means of opportunity to turn to the One Who is beyond all Causalities, but the Cause of all Causalities, Musabbabul-Asbāb Allah ﷻ.

---

36. And to Allah belongs whatever is in the heavens and whatever is on the earth. He forgives whom He wills and punishes whom He wills. And Allah is Forgiving and Merciful.
37. Degrees [of high position] from Him and forgiveness and mercy. And Allah is ever Forgiving and Merciful.

اَللهُمَّ صَلِّ عَلَى سَيِّدِنَا وَ حَبِيْبِنَا مُحَمَّد ﷺ

Allahumma Salli Ala Sayyidina wa Habibìna Muhammad ﷺ.

Juz 4

Sûrah 3 Āl-'Imrān

[64]³⁸

Adab, Critical Thinking and Learning from Each Other

قُلْ يَا أَهْلَ الْكِتَابِ تَعَالَوْاْ إِلَى كَلَمَةٍ سَوَاء بَيْنَنَا وَبَيْنَكُمْ أَلاَّ نَعْبُدَ إِلاَّ اللّهَ وَلاَ نُشْرِكَ بِهِ شَيْئًا وَلاَ يَتَّخِذَ بَعْضُنَا بَعْضاً أَرْبَابًا مِّن دُونِ اللّهِ فَإِن تَوَلَّوْاْ فَقُولُواْ اشْهَدُواْ بِأَنَّا مُسْلِمُونَ {اۤل عمران/64}

One should remember that Allah ﷻ sent other prophets starting from Adam as. In this regard, one should know the people of the Book, referred as ahlu-kitāb in the Qurān expected to know the Divine teachings as their prophets and scriptures taught them.

One of the hikmahs of the Qurān and Rasulullah ﷺ is to remind them the original teachings of Allah ﷻ as mentioned in their books, filter and remove the teachings that were not in these original teachings and lastly, show a way of life compatible with their own original teachings of the previous prophets and scriptures in an easier and applicable way according to our times until end of days.

One can witness today that Muslims are struggling today to display the core values of imān, tawhid, Islām and ihsān. The cultural values exposed on the core values of Islām, imān and ihsān seem to alienate today Muslims from their religion especially with the increasing communication systems of social media, internet, and instant communication tools.

In the past, the localization of the problem in a region due to the misinterpretation of the religion with 'urf or culture was only at a specific space. Today, with the immediate mass communication tools and empowerment of the Shayātin from humans and others, a person

---

38. Say, "O People of the Scripture, come to a word that is equitable between us and you - that we will not worship except Allah and not associate anything with Him and not take one another as lords instead of Allah." But if they turn away, then say, "Bear witness that we are Muslims [submitting to Him]."

hearing a news in one part of the world without knowing the context and verifying its source seem to be affected especially in the discourses of religious identity.

On the other hand, in this globalized world, the boundaries of adab is lifted with the promotion of critical thinking as constantly instilled in the colleges as a way of methodology of a free-man. This notion was at one point only promoted in the West. Yet, with the globalization of communication, now almost all the world is under the same flow of critical thinking as a tainted representation of free will.

There is nothing wrong with critical thinking and it should be there. Yet, our critical thinking in our tradition of true Islām as instilled by all the prophets displays itself with adab.

This challenge has been faced by all the people of the Book referred as ahlu-kitāb.

The main question is how to adapt or continue with religious identity with the changing norms and pushes of the society as sometimes understood a "spirit of rebellion" against all the given values in the family, and in the religion.

One should realize that Westerners as the frontiers of these critical thinking movements faced first this type of religious identity struggles. In other words, ahlu-kitāb faced this difficulty of holding one's religious identity against the movements of religious identity of tainted critical-thinking first.

Regardless of their methods were successful or not, one should realize that ahlu-kitāb started with different methodologies or systems to hold or generate programs, curriculums, and institutions in order not to be fully lost in the Western trends of tainted critical thinking as constantly promoted in higher level education systems.

Therefore, it is important for Muslims to analyze and study these already existing survival struggles of ahlu-kitāb with these globalized trends of critical thinking, self-identity, freedom, free-will, and religious identity. Studying does not decrease the value but can give the people better understanding of the methods of the delivery of the diamond and pearl valued teachings of the Qurān and sunnah of Rasulullah ﷺ.

As we are in a very interesting threshold with the virtual learning environments connecting all the worlds in one's kitchen table or sofas, there can be somehow similarity between this time and the time of interaction in 11ᵗʰ and 12ᵗʰ centuries especially in the regions of Andulus between Imam Ghazali (رحمه الله), Thomas Aquinous, and Meimonieds. A similar trend was the Greek philosophy affecting the religious teachings and religious identities. One can find similar interactions of revival of religions with religious identities between Imam Ghazali (رحمه الله), Thomas Aquinous, and Meimonieds. Allahu A'lam.

Adab with Allah ﷻ, adab with Rasulullah ﷺ, adab with all the prophets and adab with anything that Allah ﷻ tells us to have respect, set our boundaries of critical thinking.

On one side, there is a reminder to hold together the primary adab of Oneness and Uniqueness of Allah ﷻ as Muslims can remind others as mentioned in the Qurān قُلْ يَا أَهْلَ الْكِتَابِ تَعَالَوْاْ إِلَى كَلَمَةٍ سَوَاء بَيْنَنَا وَبَيْنَكُمْ أَلاَّ نَعْبُدَ إِلاَّ اللهَ وَلاَ نُشْرِكَ بِهِ شَيْئًا

On the other hand, Muslims can learn from ahlu-kitab the successful and failed practices of delivery of methodologies in today's struggle of survival of religious identities in promoted definitions of critical thinking, self-identity, freedom, free-will and religious identity as ahlu-kitāb first encountered these problems first in their origination of these ideas in their homelands. Allahu A'lam.

أَللهُمَّ صَلِّ على سَيِّدَنا وحَبِيْبِنَا مُحَمَّد ﷺ كَمَا صَلَّيْتَ على سَيِّدنا إبراهيم

Allahumma Salli A'la Sayyidina wa Habìbina Muhammad ﷺ Kama Sallayta a'lā Sayyidinā Ibrāhìm.

[135][39]

Levels of Nafs, Realities of Trials and the Need of Immediate Rush to Allah ﷻ

وَالَّذِينَ إِذَا فَعَلُواْ فَاحِشَةً أَوْ ظَلَمُواْ أَنْفُسَهُمْ ذَكَرُواْ اللَّهَ فَاسْتَغْفَرُواْ لِذُنُوبِهِمْ وَمَن يَغْفِرُ الذُّنُوبَ إِلاَّ اللَّهُ وَلَمْ يُصِرُّواْ عَلَى مَا فَعَلُواْ وَهُمْ يَعْلَمُونَ

{أل عمران/135}

One should remember that not accepting one's mistakes is due to hardened ego of the person.

---

39. And those who, when they commit an immorality or wrong themselves [by transgression], remember Allah and seek forgiveness for their sins - and who can forgive sins except Allah? - and [who] do not persist in what they have done while they know.

Ego or the nafs reaches at such an extreme that in the language of this person, the expressions such as "I am sorry, it was my mistake, I apologize, or please forgive me, " do not exist.

Saying these expressions are so difficult for the person that even he or she does not think the possibility of a mistake on one's part.

One can compare the two cases as between Adam as and Shaytān as:

قَالاَ رَبَّنَا ظَلَمْنَا أَنفُسَنَا وَإِن لَّمْ تَغْفِرْ لَنَا وَتَرْحَمْنَا لَنَكُونَنَّ مِنَ الْخَاسِرِينَ

{الأعراف/23}[40]

قَالَ فَبِعِزَّتِكَ لَأُغْوِيَنَّهُمْ أَجْمَعِينَ

{ص/82}[41]

One is Adam (عليه السلام). He as immediately turns to Allah ﷻ with the acceptance of mistakes and faults as mentioned ظَلَمْنَا.

The other is Shaytān. He increases in non-acceptance and going further in extremity of rejection, aggravation, mischief and misguidance.

If one carefully analyzes the Qurān the immediate turn of the person to Allah ﷻ asking forgiveness due to any possible zulm, oppression and injustice is the attitude of a person of the imān. We can witness this in the case of Adam as mentioned. We can witness in the case of Musa as with the same expression as ظَلَمْتُ in[42] قَالَ رَبِّ إِنِّي ظَلَمْتُ نَفْسِي فَاغْفِرْ لِي فَغَفَرَ لَهُ إِنَّهُ هُوَ الْغَفُورُ الرَّحِيمُ {القصص/16}. This was when Musa as accidently killed a person.

On the other, as the person waits but does not turn to Allah ﷻ, asking forgiveness and accordingly asking forgiveness from the effected people, then this regret does not seem to have much benefit. For example,[43] فَلَمَّا

---

40. They said, "Our Lord, we have wronged ourselves, and if You do not forgive us and have mercy upon us, we will surely be among the losers."

41. [Iblees] said, "By your might, I will surely mislead them all

42. He said, "My Lord, indeed I have wronged myself, so forgive me," and He forgave him. Indeed, He is the Forgiving, the Merciful.

43. **[21:12]** And when its inhabitants perceived Our punishment, at once they fled from it. **[21:13]**[Some angels said], "Do not flee but return to where you were given luxury and to your homes - perhaps you will be questioned."**[21:14]** They said, "O woe to us! Indeed, we were wrongdoers."**[21:15]**And that declaration of theirs did not cease until We made them [as] a harvest [mowed down], extinguished [like a fire].

أَحَسُّوا بَأْسَنَا إِذَا هُم مِّنْهَا يَرْكُضُونَ {الأنبياء/12} لَا تَرْكُضُوا وَارْجِعُوا إِلَى مَا أُتْرِفْتُمْ فِيهِ
وَمَسَاكِنِكُمْ لَعَلَّكُمْ تُسْأَلُونَ {الأنبياء/13} قَالُوا يَا وَيْلَنَا إِنَّا كُنَّا ظَالِمِينَ {الأنبياء/14} فَمَا زَالَت
تِّلْكَ دَعْوَاهُمْ حَتَّى جَعَلْنَاهُمْ حَصِيدًا خَامِدِينَ {الأنبياء/15}.

They also admit that they were wrong doers as mentioned قَالُوا يَا وَيْلَنَا
إِنَّا كُنَّا ظَالِمِينَ {الأنبياء/14}

Yet, it is too late, May Allah ﷻ protect us.

Now, one can think the extremity of Shaytān that after thousands or millions of years, still Shaytān does not go back and ask forgiveness from Allah ﷻ. In fact, there is a story about Shaytān and Musa as that Musa as tells Shaytān that he as can ask forgiveness for him from Allah ﷻ. Then, Musa as asks Allah ﷻ and then, the condition of forgiveness for Shaytān is to go the grave of Adam as to make sajdah in order to respect him. Then, Shaytān says "I didn't respect him and make sajdah when he was alive. Now, why should I make sajdah to his dead body?" Astagfirullah,

May Allah ﷻ protect us from the hardened position of our nafs avoiding to ask forgiveness from Allah ﷻ and accordingly from people.

The notion of popularized term in Islamic writings as "nafsul firawniyah" represents this hardened ego or nafs of the person that does not accept any blame or mistake and does not want to ask forgiveness. In this regard, the prototype of Fir'awn in the Qurān can represent constant rejection of the message of Musa (عليه السلام), when many times the message presented to him in different formats and forms as ayah, signs, reasonings, and logic. Yet, he refused. Therefore, this term became popular among Islamic scholars to represent another hardened position of the nafs-ego.

In this regard, if one really depicts a chart in the negativity and hardened forms of nafs, an example can be

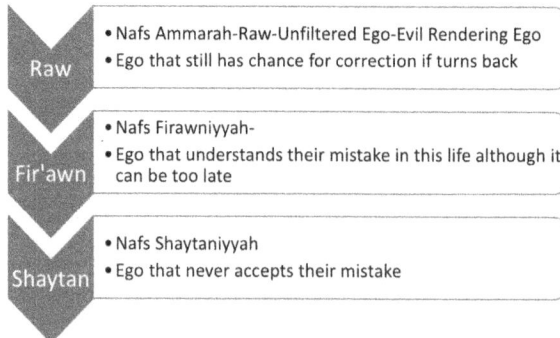

Raw	• Nafs Ammarah-Raw-Unfiltered Ego-Evil Rendering Ego • Ego that still has chance for correction if turns back
Fir'awn	• Nafs Firawniyyah- • Ego that understands their mistake in this life although it can be too late
Shaytan	• Nafs Shaytaniyyah • Ego that never accepts their mistake

On the other hand, the people of imān do not insist in their mistakes and immediately and ask forgiveness from Allah ﷻ and from people. This is mentioned as[44] وَالَّذِينَ إِذَا فَعَلُواْ فَاحِشَةً أَوْ ظَلَمُواْ أَنْفُسَهُمْ ذَكَرُواْ اللّهَ فَاسْتَغْفَرُواْ لِذُنُوبِهِمْ وَمَن يَغْفِرُ الذُّنُوبَ إِلاَّ اللّهُ وَلَمْ يُصِرُّواْ عَلَى مَا فَعَلُواْ وَهُمْ يَعْلَمُونَ {آل عمران/135}

A person of imān do not insist with mistakes as mentioned وَلَمْ يُصِرُّواْ وَلَمْ يُصِرُّواْ عَلَى مَا . SubhanAllah! This expression عَلَى مَا فَعَلُواْ وَهُمْ يَعْلَمُونَ exactly represents purposeful insistence on a mistake and leading the nafs passing from nafs ammarah to nafs firawniyyah and nafs Shaytaniyyah. May Allah ﷻ protect us, Amin. The key is the insistence on a mistake, oppression, abuse and anything displeasing Allah ﷻ, Astagfirullah.

The more the person waits the difficult it becomes for the person to accept one's mistake and turn to Allah ﷻ and ask forgiveness. Therefore, in the renderings of possible mistakes, sins, errors, abuse or oppression, one should be in the rushing mode to ask forgiveness. The upper limit of three days about not talking to a person as set by Rasulullah [10] ﷺ 14]] can eliminate the possible hardening of nafs passing to stages of firawniyyah and Shaytaniyyah, may Allah ﷻ protect us, Amin.

This is a very serious matter. One should really not take it as a joke and play around it. In each disposition of hardening of nafs, there is an indication of displeasure of Allah ﷻ, may Allah ﷻ protect us.

Each hardened nafs claim deity in its disposition running against the reality of La ilaha illa Allah although he or she may verbally utter this sacred and blessed phrase.

Each liquid nafs changing form and dissolving itself in the reality of La ilaha illa Allah represents the nafs of the person of imān.

Each vaporized nafs from liquid state represent the imān of the elect such as the prophets, as.

---

44. And those who, when they commit an immorality or wrong themselves [by transgression], remember Allah and seek forgiveness for their sins - and who can forgive sins except Allah? - and [who] do not persist in what they have done while they know.

One can view the chart below in this regard:

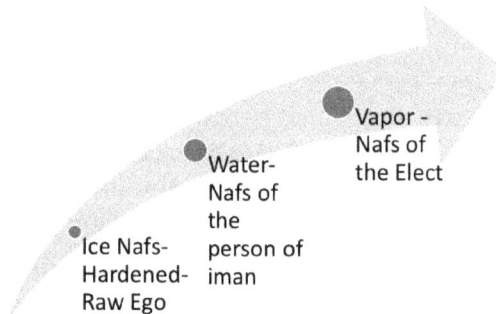

Vapor -
Nafs of
the Elect

Water-
Nafs of
the
Ice Nafs-   person of
Hardened-   iman
Raw Ego

In the above depiction of nafs, one can realize, the more there is the degrees of freedom of molecules as mentioned in physics from solid, to liquid and then to gas state, then the further volatility and flexibility increase. Similarly, acceptance one's mistake's is flexibility and destroying the solid and hardened state of the nafs.

One can remember the analogy of Rasulullah (salallahu alayhi wasallam) [10] that a kafir is similar to a solid tree that does not seem to be affected with the wind. A punishing storm can take out this tree from its roots. A mu'min, a person of imãn, is similar to a bending plant that swings with the wind but comes back to its position.

SubhanAllah!

In this regard, a kafir can seem to have very strong personality. A person of hardened nafs can seem to have very strong oppressing personality without accepting any self-blame. Yet, a strong wind as a punishment can knock down this tree and displaying the real position of the kafir in the akhirah and in this life. May Allah ﷻ, protect us.

On the other hand, a person of imãn, can show the attitude of humbleness and humility and readiness to accept one's mistakes. By accepting one's mistakes, he may seem to be bending down but yet, it is a power of humility that the person receives from Allah ﷻ going back to his or her equilibrium position of being a'bd of Allah ﷻ. This is similar to the position of a string with its potential energy in physics.

Raw nafs never want to accept its mistake. Especially, as time passes from the incident of a trial or test, it hardens and hardens until it revolves around its deity of self-gratification and self-idolatry. Astagfirullah, may Allah ﷻ protect us, Amìn.

The person of imãn rushes to make tawbah as mentioned a case of a possible mistake for Dawûd alayhis salam[45] وَظَنَّ دَاوُودُ أَنَّمَا فَتَنَّاهُ فَاسْتَغْفَرَ رَبَّهُ وَخَرَّ رَاكِعًا وَأَنَابَ {ص/24} The selection of the verses in this ayah is amazing. The word ظَنَّ can indicate a possibility of a mistake. The word وَخَرَّ can indicate the attitude and mode of rushing to ask forgiveness from Allah ﷻ. So, Dawûd (عليه السلام) did not wait but immediately rush to Allah ﷻ for a possibility of a mistake, Allahumma Ja'alna minhum, Amìn.

One should remember most of the time our frustrations in life occur due to the expectations from people. Then, the person attracts trials and tests in these relationships. This is so true!

One should realize that the purpose of trials and tests are to break and destroy these pseudo and false expectations and dependencies of the person on everything except Allah ﷻ.

This dependency can also be a pious wife, a supporting relative or anything.

It is mentioned that one of the sabab nuzûl of Sûrah Duha is to teach this reality with the life of Rasulullah ﷺ, al-Habìb ﷺ. Although there is no dependency of Rasulullah ﷺ except to Allah ﷻ, yet losing his ﷺ beloved wife, our mother Khadija (رضي الله عنها) and his uncle as his supporter at a time of an extreme execution can also help us to reconsider our relationship with Allah ﷻ.

Yes, as humans we get affected and build relationships with the people that we much spend time with. Yet, regardless of who they are, our hearts really bleed spiritually when there are tests and trials evolving around the loved ones, May Allah ﷻ protect us, Amìn.

One should leave all the spiritual and physical dependencies except Allah ﷻ before they leave us with pain, agony, and tears.

أَللّٰهُمَّ صَلِّ على سَيِّدَنا وحَبِيْبِنَا مُحَمَّد ﷺ

Allahumma Salli Ala Sayyidina wa Habibina Muhammad ﷺ

Heedlessness-Gaflah, Oppression-Dhulm and Balance

وَالَّذِينَ إِذَا فَعَلُواْ فَاحِشَةً أَوْ ظَلَمُواْ أَنْفُسَهُمْ ذَكَرُواْ اللهَ فَاسْتَغْفَرُواْ لِذُنُوبِهِمْ وَمَن يَغْفِرُ الذُّنُوبَ إِلاَّ اللهُ وَلَمْ يُصِرُّواْ عَلَى مَا فَعَلُواْ وَهُمْ يَعْلَمُونَ {آل عمران/135}[46]

---

45. And David became certain that We had tried him, and he asked forgiveness of his Lord and fell down bowing [in prostration] and turned in repentance [to Allah].

46. And those who, when they commit an immorality or wrong themselves [by transgression], remember Allah and seek forgiveness for their sins – and who can forgive sins except Allah? – and [who] do not persist in what they have done while they know.

One should remember that Allah ﷻ is the only One that one can find constant relief and stability of the heart. Sometimes, our humanly needs block us in the overindulgence of that need by being in the states of gaflah-heedlessness with our relationships with Allah ﷻ.

Yet, every gaflah-heedlessness and every imbalance due to overindulgence have their own side effects.

This can be a similar to a patient going for chemotherapy. Then, he gains weight due its side effects of this treatment and now, he needs to deal with other problems such as heart disease, high cholesterol, and others.

It is very difficult to keep the balance once we are involved in something.

Especially, if this involvement is due to the urges of our humanly needs.

People of the heart referred as ahlullah or people of Allah ﷻ always look at their heart and intention before, during, and after their involvement with an action.

If there are imbalances, they immediately run to Allah ﷻ with istighfār, and asking forgiveness to reset themselves with Allah ﷻ.

Every imbalance can cause evil on the self and others if it is not reset with Allah ﷻ.

Every overindulgence without balance can cause instability of the heart and mind on oneself. One can call this dhulm-oppression of the person on their own selves. The Qurān mentions the personal self-oppression engagements constantly. When the person oppresses oneself referred as dhulm, then oppression becomes normalized. Then, he or she finds avenues of oppression for others starting with the immediate ones, such as the spouses, children, parents, siblings, friends or others as much as he or she can extend.

May Allah ﷻ protect us the instabilities of the heart and mind causing oppression-dhulm on ourselves and others, Amìn.

May Allah ﷻ give us the ability of running back to Allah ﷻ in our oppression to reset ourselves with istighfār, and asking forgiveness, Amìn.

أَللهُمَّ صَلِّ على سَيِّدَنا وحَبِيْبَنا مُحَمَّد ﷺ

Allahumma Salli a'la Sayyidina wa Habìbina Muhammad ﷺ

[159]

The Applicability of Take-in & Dissolve System against Harsh & Rude Treatments

وَعِبَادُ الرَّحْمَنِ الَّذِينَ يَمْشُونَ عَلَى الْأَرْضِ هَوْنًا وَإِذَا خَاطَبَهُمُ الْجَاهِلُونَ قَالُوا سَلَامًا
{الفرقان/63}[47]

وَمَا أَرْسَلْنَاكَ إِلَّا رَحْمَةً لِّلْعَالَمِينَ
{الأنبياء/107}[48]

فَبِمَا رَحْمَةٍ مِّنَ اللّهِ لِنتَ لَهُمْ وَلَوْ كُنتَ فَظًّا غَلِيظَ الْقَلْبِ لَانفَضُّواْ مِنْ حَوْلِكَ فَاعْفُ عَنْهُمْ وَاسْتَغْفِرْ لَهُمْ وَشَاوِرْهُمْ فِي الأَمْرِ فَإِذَا عَزَمْتَ فَتَوَكَّلْ عَلَى اللّهِ إِنَّ اللّهَ يُحِبُّ الْمُتَوَكِّلِينَ
{آل عمران/159}[49]

One should know that Allah ﷻ is al-Gafur al Rahìm- the Most Forgiving, the Most Merciful. Although we deserve a lot of retribution in our evil renderings, Allah ﷻ does not retribute us, SubhanAllah.

On the other hand, we cannot even take a word that is unjustly or improperly said to us, SubhanAllah.

The maqāmat of the person with Allah ﷻ displays how much he or she takes in and dissolves them without any harm in oneself.

Today, we have fields or disciplines which deal with the people who cannot take in and dissolve. Psychology, psychiatry, social work or counseling are some of them.

Yet, the levels of take in and dissolve exist in the person for the sake of Allah ﷻ not for anything else.

One can remember the famous incident of Rumi (رحمه الله) when he was cursed on his face for a few minutes by a person who was a Muslim due to his welcoming attitude for all faiths regardless of their faith. Rumi (رحمه الله) listened to him smiling until he was done with his curses to his. Then, Rumi (رحمه الله)said "are you done?", the man said "yes," then Rumi (رحمه الله) stepped forward, hugged him and said "we welcome you with love too."

---

47. And the servants of the Most Merciful are those who walk upon the earth easily, and when the ignorant address them [harshly], they say [words of] peace (salam).
48. And We have not sent you, [O Muhammad], except as a mercy to the worlds.
49. So, by mercy from Allah, [O Muhammad], you were lenient with them. And if you had been rude [in speech] and harsh in heart, they would have disbanded from about you. So, pardon them and ask forgiveness for them and consult them in the matter. And when you have decided, then rely upon Allah. Indeed, Allah loves those who rely [upon Him].

It is very difficult to implement the notion take in and dissolve without spiritual self-destruction. We are at a time that the approach of take in—dissolve can be also viewed as abuse, weakness or losing self-confidence.

According to people of the heart and mind, the level of ihsān or patience is not presence when you don't have the means. The levels of ihsān or patience-sabr is present when you have the means to take revenge and retribute, but you don't take revenge or retribute but you handle the cases with wisdom-hikmah and sabr-patience.

One of the prominent Names and Attributes of Allah ﷻ is al-Sābur, the One Who is Patient. Allah ﷻ can destroy us at any time with any means or without any means. Yet, Allah ﷻ is al-Gafûr and al-Rahìm, the Most Forgiving, the Most Merciful.

In one of the narrations from Rasulullah ﷺ mentioned to emulate the reflection of Attributes of Allah ﷻ in one's character building.

The Qurān praises the high characters of all the prophets Ibrāhim (عليه السلام), Musa (عليه السلام), Isa (عليه السلام), all others and Rasulullah ﷺ-the Prophet Muhammad ﷺ. The Qurān mentions specifically the character of Rasulullah ﷺ that if he ﷺ was harsh, everyone would disappear from around him. Yet, he ﷺ was extremely gentle, soft and kind implementing the take in-dissolve fully and perfectly. One can see this approach in all the role models as we call them prophets and messengers, or teachers.

اللهُمَّ صَلِّ عَلَى سَيِّدِنَا وَ حَبِيْبِنَا مُحَمّد ﷺ وعلى آله وصحبه وسلم

Allahumma Salli A'la Sayyidina wa Habibina Muhammad ﷺ wa a'lā a'lihi wa sahbihi wa Sallim.

Juz 5

Sûrah 4 al-Nisã

[140]

Unpleasant Environments of Gathering

وَقَدْ نَزَّلَ عَلَيْكُمْ فِي الْكِتَابِ أَنْ إِذَا سَمِعْتُمْ آيَاتِ اللَّهِ يُكَفَرُ بِهَا وَيُسْتَهْزَأُ بِهَا فَلاَ تَقْعُدُواْ مَعَهُمْ حَتَّى يَخُوضُواْ فِي حَدِيثٍ غَيْرِهِ إِنَّكُمْ إِذًا مِّثْلُهُمْ إِنَّ اللَّهَ جَامِعُ الْمُنَافِقِينَ وَالْكَافِرِينَ فِي جَهَنَّمَ جَمِيعًا
{النساء/140}[50]

وَمِنَ النَّاسِ مَن يَشْتَرِي لَهْوَ الْحَدِيثِ لِيُضِلَّ عَن سَبِيلِ اللَّهِ بِغَيْرِ عِلْمٍ وَيَتَّخِذَهَا هُزُوًا أُوْلَئِكَ لَهُمْ عَذَابٌ مُّهِينٌ

{لقمان/6}[51]

وَإِذَا رَأَيْتَ الَّذِينَ يَخُوضُونَ فِي آيَاتِنَا فَأَعْرِضْ عَنْهُمْ حَتَّى يَخُوضُواْ فِي حَدِيثٍ غَيْرِهِ وَإِمَّا يُنسِيَنَّكَ الشَّيْطَانُ فَلاَ تَقْعُدْ بَعْدَ الذِّكْرَى مَعَ الْقَوْمِ الظَّالِمِينَ
{الأنعام/68}[52]

وَإِذَا ذُكِرَ اللَّهُ وَحْدَهُ اشْمَأَزَّتْ قُلُوبُ الَّذِينَ لاَ يُؤْمِنُونَ بِالآخِرَةِ وَإِذَا ذُكِرَ الَّذِينَ مِن دُونِهِ إِذَا هُمْ يَسْتَبْشِرُونَ
{الزمر/45}[53]

One should remember that Allah ﷻ is aware of our hearts and minds. When a person is in gatherings with people who may not have a genuine

---

50. And it has already come down to you in the Book that when you hear the verses of Allah [recited], they are denied [by them] and ridiculed; so do not sit with them until they enter into another conversation. Indeed, you would then be like them. Indeed Allah will gather the hypocrites and disbelievers in Hell all together -

51. And of the people is he who buys the amusement of speech to mislead [others] from the way of Allah without knowledge and who takes it in ridicule. Those will have a humiliating punishment.

52. And when you see those who engage in [offensive] discourse concerning Our verses, then turn away from them until they enter into another conversation. And if Satan should cause you to forget, then do not remain after the reminder with the wrongdoing people.

53. And when Allah is mentioned alone, the hearts of those who do not believe in the Hereafter shrink with aversion, but when those [worshipped] other than Him are mentioned, immediately they rejoice.

relationship with Allah ﷻ, our hearts, emotions, and thoughts can be affected.

These sometimes unpleasant and unfulfilling effects can make the person uncomfortable. Yet, always the remedy and cure is to run back to Allah ﷻ with dua, istighfãr, asking help and 'iãna from Allah ﷻ.

Sometimes, the source of discomfort is due to the talks about the criticizing the friends of Allah ﷻ. A person with only a secular mindset of intellect as a Muslim void of proper adab with ahlullah can hurt and disturb the ones who have a genuine relationship with Allah ﷻ and accordingly have adab with ahlullah.

Even if these negative talks and engagements are related with the messengers of Allah ﷻ, the scriptures and about the One who gave the person everything, the level of disturbance in a genuine person of imãn can be at the highest level with extreme discomfort and repulsion as if the person is running out from this environment to throw up.

One should remember that a person who doesn't know Allah ﷻ and not a Muslim can have a normal disposition of lack of knowledge and hidayah.

A person who is a Muslim presenting these diseases can make the person more uncomfortable due to some minimum expectations of the shi'ar of Islãm this person is expected to follow.

We have a lot of diseases in our hearts affecting our imãn. When a person has a disease in his or her tongue, they cannot taste the sweetness of honey. One can try to rationalize with all logical arguments the sweet taste of honey for the person who is diseased in his or her tongue, yet it is very difficult for this person to understand fully this sweetness unless this disease is removed, and the person can feel and experience it.

Similarly, the diseases around our imãn make us not to the taste the real sweetness of imãn which is sweeter than a honey. One should work on oneself with tazkiyatul nafs, removal of these diseases to taste this sweetness. The sole logical and intellectual arguments is not sufficient to remove the diseases. May Allah ﷻ protect us but sometimes an evil-seeming incident in a person's life can make a painful surgery for tazkiyatul nafs removing the attachments in one's heart and cleaning the diseases with hardened tumors around imãn.

Even sometimes, genuine Muslims can have the engagements of a wrong time, topic, or place for the true embodiment of Dhikrullah with the true context as mentioned[54]

يَا أَيُّهَا الَّذِينَ آمَنُوا لَا تَدْخُلُوا بُيُوتَ النَّبِيِّ إِلَّا أَن يُؤْذَنَ لَكُمْ إِلَى طَعَامٍ غَيْرَ نَاظِرِينَ إِنَاهُ وَلَكِنْ إِذَا دُعِيتُمْ فَادْخُلُوا فَإِذَا طَعِمْتُمْ فَانتَشِرُوا وَلَا مُسْتَأْنِسِينَ لِحَدِيثٍ إِنَّ ذَلِكُمْ كَانَ يُؤْذِي النَّبِيَّ فَيَسْتَحْيِي مِنكُمْ وَاللَّهُ لَا يَسْتَحْيِي مِنَ الْحَقِّ وَإِذَا سَأَلْتُمُوهُنَّ مَتَاعًا فَاسْأَلُوهُنَّ مِن وَرَاءِ حِجَابٍ ذَلِكُمْ أَطْهَرُ لِقُلُوبِكُمْ وَقُلُوبِهِنَّ وَمَا كَانَ لَكُمْ أَن تُؤْذُوا رَسُولَ اللَّهِ وَلَا أَن تَنكِحُوا أَزْوَاجَهُ مِن بَعْدِهِ أَبَدًا إِنَّ ذَلِكُمْ كَانَ عِندَ اللَّهِ عَظِيمًا {الأحزاب/53}

May Allah ﷻ protect us, the matter is serious. There is the displeasure of Allah ﷻ and Rasulullah ﷺ.

Yet, in all cases, we should maintain our judgment free disposition but adapt self-care mode of protection not to be affected with these diseases by constantly running back to Allah ﷻ with dua and istighfār.

At the same time, one should constantly ask hidayah, protection for oneself and for others on the path of Allah ﷻ and Rasulullah ﷺ.

اللهُمَّ صَلِّ عَلَى سَيِّدِنَا وَ حَبِيبِنَا مُحَمَّد ﷺ

Allahumma Salli a'la Sayyidina wa Habibina Muhammad ﷺ

Juz 6

Sûrah 5 al-Māidah

[54][55]

Replacement of Groups & Deadly Group Identities

يَا أَيُّهَا الَّذِينَ آمَنُوا مَن يَرْتَدَّ مِنكُمْ عَن دِينِهِ فَسَوْفَ يَأْتِي اللَّهُ بِقَوْمٍ يُحِبُّهُمْ وَيُحِبُّونَهُ أَذِلَّةٍ عَلَى الْمُؤْمِنِينَ أَعِزَّةٍ عَلَى الْكَافِرِينَ يُجَاهِدُونَ فِي سَبِيلِ اللَّهِ وَلَا يَخَافُونَ لَوْمَةَ لَائِمٍ ذَلِكَ فَضْلُ اللَّهِ يُؤْتِيهِ مَن يَشَاءُ وَاللَّهُ وَاسِعٌ عَلِيمٌ {المائدة/54}

---

54. O you who have believed, do not enter the houses of the Prophet except when you are permitted for a meal, without awaiting its readiness. But when you are invited, then enter; and when you have eaten, disperse without seeking to remain for conversation. Indeed, that [behavior] was troubling the Prophet, and he is shy of [dismissing] you. But Allah is not shy of the truth. And when you ask [his wives] for something, ask them from behind a partition. That is purer for your hearts and their hearts. And it is not [conceivable or lawful] for you to harm the Messenger of Allah or to marry his wives after him, ever. Indeed, that would be in the sight of Allah an enormity.

55. O you who have believed, whoever of you should revert from his religion - Allah will bring forth [in place of them] a people He will love and who will love Him [who are] humble toward the believers, powerful against the disbelievers; they strive in the cause of Allah and do not fear the blame of a critic. That is the favor of Allah; He bestows it upon whom He wills. And Allah is all-Encompassing and Knowing.

يَا أَيُّهَا الَّذِينَ آمَنُواْ مَا لَكُمْ إِذَا قِيلَ لَكُمُ انفِرُواْ فِي سَبِيلِ اللهِ اثَّاقَلْتُمْ إِلَى الأَرْضِ أَرَضِيتُم بِالْحَيَاةِ الدُّنْيَا مِنَ الآخِرَةِ فَمَا مَتَاعُ الْحَيَاةِ الدُّنْيَا فِي الآخِرَةِ إِلاَّ قَلِيلٌ {التوبة/38}[56] إِلاَّ تَنفِرُواْ يُعَذِّبْكُمْ عَذَابًا أَلِيمًا وَيَسْتَبْدِلْ قَوْمًا غَيْرَكُمْ وَلاَ تَضُرُّوهُ شَيْئًا وَاللهُ عَلَى كُلِّ شَيْءٍ قَدِيرٌ {التوبة/39}[57]

هَاأَنتُمْ هَؤُلاء تُدْعَوْنَ لِتُنفِقُوا فِي سَبِيلِ اللهِ فَمِنكُم مَّن يَبْخَلُ وَمَن يَبْخَلْ فَإِنَّمَا يَبْخَلُ عَن نَّفْسِهِ وَاللَّهُ الْغَنِيُّ وَأَنتُمُ الْفُقَرَاء وَإِن تَتَوَلَّوْا يَسْتَبْدِلْ قَوْمًا غَيْرَكُمْ ثُمَّ لَا يَكُونُوا أَمْثَالَكُمْ {محمد/38}[58]

One should focus the critical expressions of the replacement of a group as mentioned in above ayahs as يُحِبُّهُمْ وَيُحِبُّونَهُ أَذِلَّةٍ عَلَى and وَيَسْتَبْدِلْ قَوْمًا غَيْرَكُمْ الْمُؤْمِنِينَ أَعِزَّةٍ عَلَى الْكَافِرِينَ.

One should remember that group identities can be killing and devastating. The only group identity that we have and always proud is being a Muslim.

Even this identity is very clearly elaborated in the Qurān that the identity of being a Muslim does not only belong to us with the religion of Islām with Rasulullah ﷺ but it was always there as an inclusive identity with other prophets and their followers such as Ibrahim (عليه السلام), Isa (عليه السلام), Yusuf (عليه السلام), Musa (عليه السلام) and others. In this regard, being a Muslim is not classical tagged club identity, but it is the purpose of life and existence as mentioned by Yusuf (عليه السلام) with the expression رَبِّ قَدْ آتَيْتَنِي مِنَ الْمُلْكِ وَعَلَّمْتَنِي مِن تَأْوِيلِ الأَحَادِيثِ تَوَفَّنِي مُسْلِمًا فَاطِرَ السَّمَاوَاتِ وَالأَرْضِ أَنتَ وَلِيِّي فِي الدُّنْيَا وَالآخِرَةِ تَوَفَّنِي مُسْلِمًا وَأَلْحِقْنِي بِالصَّالِحِينَ {يوسف/101}[59].

---

56. O you who have believed, what is [the matter] with you that, when you are told to go forth in the cause of Allah, you adhere heavily to the earth? Are you satisfied with the life of this world rather than the Hereafter? But what is the enjoyment of worldly life compared to the Hereafter except a [very] little.

57. If you do not go forth, He will punish you with a painful punishment and will replace you with another people, and you will not harm Him at all. And Allah is over all things competent.

58. Here you are - those invited to spend in the cause of Allah - but among you are those who withhold [out of greed]. And whoever withholds only withholds [benefit] from himself; and Allah is the Free of need, while you are the needy. And if you turn away, He will replace you with another people; then they will not be the likes of you.

59. My Lord, You have given me [something] of sovereignty and taught me of the interpretation of dreams. Creator of the heavens and earth, You are my protector in this world and in the Hereafter. Cause me to die a Muslim and join me with the righteous."

In this regard, one really tragically smile and feel sad when the person constantly witness these killing group identities as a X group, Y group movement, Z mosque community and etc.

Naming something as a group and moving with people along to a goal on the path of Allah ﷻ is a virtue.

Yet, if this group is not constantly reminded to reset this identity to a zero level as a pseudo and fake hindering identity in the realities of a being a humble a'bd as a Muslim in front of Allah ﷻ, then this engagement can be test for the group, the individuals in the group and the group leads. May Allah ﷻ protect us, Amìn.

One of the signs of a healthy group movement is support all the virtuous actions outside the group, encourage them and be involved in their formation. If the group has an approach such that "if our group did not start this initiative or if our does not fully own this action, then we are not involved", then these are signs of a diseased group engagement, which can attract the displeasure of Allah ﷻ with trials and tests leading to earthquakes shaking the group and group movement with a possible destruction. May Allah ﷻ protect us, Amìn.

Sometimes, Allah ﷻ can give openings to a group and uphold them in integrity due to their certain practice that Allah ﷻ can be pleased much.

This can be the group's engagement in the love of Rasulullah ﷺ and its teachings and reminders around it. Due this engagement, Allah ﷻ can open the doors of a lot of khayr.

Another can be the group's enagement in one of the practices of Rasulullah ﷺ such as making good mashawarah-istisharah in decision making not promoting superiority of the self, or a charismatic leader. This indicate being a true a'bd in front of Allah ﷻ. Due this engagement, Allah ﷻ can open the doors of a lot of khayr.

There can be other specific virtues of a group that can uphold the continuity of the group. The pleasure of Allah ﷻ always embeded in practices of Rasulullah ﷺ.

Yet, when the group identities become much more pronounced beyond being a simple a'bd of Allah ﷻ with humbleness and humility in front of Allah ﷻ as a Muslim, then May Allah ﷻ protect us, there can be trials or tests, Allahu A'lam.

One should remember that when a person is in their death bed, the only meaningful group identity is being a Muslim as pillar at its essential and foundational level. Yet, being in a group and working together is very critical and important. Yet, in our self-accountability of resetting ourselves daily and constantly, our real identity forms when we are Muslim in front of Allah ﷻ as an individual as an a'bd. Therefore, implying our arrogance of self-ego-nafs, embedded in group identities of matter such as being a fire vs mud, color being white vs black, ethnicity being Arab vs non-Arab, country being American vs non-American, all with others can be deadly on the true path of Allah ﷻ.

Astagfirullah!

May Allah ﷻ protect us from our own selves, Amìn

May Allah ﷻ make us follow the path of Rasulullah ﷺ, Amìn

اللهُمَّ صَلِّ عَلَى سَيِّدِنَا وَ حَبِيْبَنَا مُحَمَّد ﷺ

Allahumma Salli Ala Sayyidina wa Habìbina Muhammad, ﷺ.

Juz 8

Sûrah 6 al-An'ãm

[116]⁶⁰

Loss of Majority, Responsibility of Authority-Parents, and Social Media-Chat Groups

وَإِن تُطِعْ أَكْثَرَ مَن فِي الأَرْضِ يُضِلُّوكَ عَن سَبِيلِ اللهِ إِن يَتَّبِعُونَ إِلاَّ الظَّنَّ وَإِنْ هُمْ إِلاَّ يَخْرُصُونَ

{الأنعام/116}

Responsibility of Authority-Parents

One should remember that Allah ﷻ is al-Gafûr al-Rahìm. Allah ﷻ can forgive any person at any time.

We should not attach ourselves anything or anyone except Allah ﷻ.

Sometimes, the people in authority positions get frustrated due to the guidelines, and rules set by this position.

In an authority position of setting guidelines, a person of imãn always prioritize the guidelines set by Allah ﷻ and Rasulullah ﷺ.

A person who in a position of decision making such as a father, a mother, or a leader in a Jam'ah can become bewildered how to guide,

---

60. And if you obey most of those upon the earth, they will mislead you from the way of Allah. They follow not except assumption, and they are not but falsifying.

apply the rules and still be in the boundaries of guidelines as set by Allah ﷻ and Rasulullah ﷺ especially when the things which were considered doubtful, makruh or even haram becomes now normalized. May Allah ﷻ protect us, Amìn.

Our own nafs with the nafs-ego of others like to bend these guidelines due to our self and personal benefits.

May Allah ﷻ protect us, Amìn.

Yet, the barakah and pleasure and protection of Allah ﷻ displays with the carefulness of these guidelines being followed by the people of imān in their personal, family, social and other lives of engagement.

One should remember holding responsibility with authority is a reality as mentioned in the Qurān[61] يَا أَيُّهَا الَّذِينَ آمَنُوا قُوا أَنفُسَكُمْ وَأَهْلِيكُمْ نَارًا وَقُودُهَا النَّاسُ وَالْحِجَارَةُ عَلَيْهَا مَلَائِكَةٌ غِلَاظٌ شِدَادٌ لَا يَعْصُونَ اللَّهَ مَا أَمَرَهُمْ وَيَفْعَلُونَ مَا يُؤْمَرُونَ {التحريم/6}.

Therefore, having constant concern about one's family members and subjects should be present. This constant concern itself is a dua to Allah ﷻ for their protection by Allah ﷻ.

أللهم جَعَلنا مِنهُم ،آمين

Allahumma Ja'alna Minhum, Amìn.

Loss of Majority & Normalizing the Makruh & Haram

Today, we see that every possible haram or doubtful item that was considered as so before tend to become halal or become normalized as as we Muslims, we seem to overlook and don't care about it.

If there are communities, groups, individuals or families that tend to still be careful in these doubtful engagements, we as Muslims label them similar to hypocrites, seeing them people of external religiosity but internally rotten, oppressor, and abuser.

Yes, we are at a time that everything is becoming upside down with social media, internet, phones, and computers. The reality of flow of majority with social media representing a loss in this life and afterlife can be viewed with the ayah[62] وَإِن تُطِعْ أَكْثَرَ مَن فِي الْأَرْضِ يُضِلُّوكَ عَن سَبِيلِ اللَّهِ إِن يَتَّبِعُونَ إِلاَّ الظَّنَّ وَإِنْ هُمْ إِلاَّ يَخْرُصُونَ {الأنعام/116}.

---

61. O you who have believed, protect yourselves and your families from a Fire whose fuel is people and stones, over which are [appointed] angels, harsh and severe; they do not disobey Allah in what He commands them but do what they are commanded.
62. And if you obey most of those upon the earth, they will mislead you from the way of Allah. They follow not except assumption, and they are not but falsifying.

One can really sympathize with Amish communities from Christians why they declared war against technological items booming with industry and technology. Then, they have established their own communities. The point here is not to be like Amish but realizing the problem is the first step.

Muslims are not fully aware of dangers of this new systems of mental and spiritual destruction of warfare through this accessible unfiltered information of mixed worldwide users.

Now, we find ourselves in the states of confusion, not knowing what is right or wrong. Since, we don't have critical judgment skills of differentiation, our confusion and blurring of the hearts and mind increase with constant bombardment of the unfiltered data by carrying cell phones next to us, then, slowly but surely all the mubham-questionable items become permissible and the items related with haram becomes normal in our daily lives with infiltration.

SubhanAllah!

Let us look at an example. A religious girl who is sensitive interacting with an opposite gender, gets a phone from her parents as a naïve gift for "protecting their daughter" and checking on her. Then, she is added to mixed gender groups of family members, cousins etc. Then, she normalizes this interaction. Then, personal chats may start. If not or together, then she starts playing an online game. She then finds others playing the same game. Then, mixed genders, Muslims and non-Muslims, they all play with inappropriate languages, curse words and others....SubhanAllah!

Now, this girl thinks that a girl who does not have phone is backwards. If she sees a religious girl with such sensitives, she sees her as a hypocrite. Because, this religious girl also considers herself as religious. What a loss!

The reason is simple. The information that is provide in this unfiltered data of different motivations such as business, marketing, advertisements or proselytizing aims. Do you think that most of them have adab with Allah ﷻ and Rasulullah ﷺ or with the sacred knowledge related with it?

We need a lot of help and we need a lot of dua that we need to make to Allah ﷻ

Chat Groups & Religious Knowledge

In my opinion, even a religious knowledge that is not presented at a right time, place and according to the specific audience and specific learning goal can increase the confused states of people.

In other words, people's membership with different religious contented chats being a platform serving a sharing as "a religious piece of knowledge" with an intention of increasing one's piety, can also increase the blurring of the minds and hearts. Because:

When a person opens a chat, the person's state of heart and mind is at a specific state at that time. So, knowledge intake really is not scheduled but randomized when the person clicks on his or her phone for that chat box. Then, this becomes an invaluable habit.

In this case, a person can be viewing sacred knowledge with an attitude of viewing a chat box. SubhanAllah!

This attitude itself can make the person be isolated from the sacred knowledge. Because sacred knowledge requires the adab of the mind and heart before, during and after its involvement. One can ask what is the difference of a philosopher without the knowledge and experience of adab with the sacred knowledge compared to a Muslim who doesn't have any adab with the sacred knowledge?

The first has more likely to be guided due to his or her unintentional or attitude with the absence of knowledge and experience of adab compared to the second case who claims that he or she knows but misguided with the sacred knowledge due to absence of adab. Allahu A'lam. May Allah ﷻ protect us, Amìn.

Another problem of these chat groups is that the randomized religious topics. The person's mind and heart swing around without focus. Marifatullah needs focus, analysis and deduction as referred as istinbāt in terminology.

A person cannot dive into the depths of knowledge of the Qurān and Sunnah of Rasulullah ﷺ through the means of chat groups and with constant distraction in lives. SubhanAllah!

May Allah ﷻ protect us and guide us for the sake of Rasulullah ﷺ, Amìn.

اَللّٰهُمَّ صَلِّ على سيدنا وحبيبنا محمد ﷺ و على آل سيدنا محمد كما صليت على سيدنا إبراهيم إنك حميد مجيد

Allahumma Salli ala Sayyidina Muhammad wa ala a'li Sayyidina Muhammad ﷺ kama sallayte a'la Sayyidina Ibrahìm wa a'la a'lì Sayyidina Ibramhìm Innaka Hamìdun Majìd.

Juz 9

Sûrah 7 al-A'râf

Spiritual Alertness of Red Zone-Tayaqquz & Middle Way-Balance- Sirât al-Mustaqìm

أَفَأَمِنُواْ مَكْرَ اللّهِ فَلاَ يَأْمَنُ مَكْرَ اللّهِ إِلاَّ الْقَوْمُ الْخَاسِرُونَ
{الأعراف/99}[63]

One should remember that our times of bast-spiritual expansion- with spiritual joy and happiness of closeness to Allah ﷻ can be an opening for trials and tests.

The reality and embodiment of tayaqquz that at any time the person can be destroyed with any try and test coming from Allah ﷻ is a reality as mentioned أَفَأَمِنُواْ مَكْرَ اللّهِ فَلاَ يَأْمَنُ مَكْرَ اللّهِ إِلاَّ الْقَوْمُ الْخَاسِرُونَ {الأعراف/99} [15].

One should remember that makr-tests and trials- coming from Allah ﷻ has a wisdom for the benefit of the person unlike the trials of humans aiming to destroy and put the person in chaotic spiritual and physical states as mentioned[64] وَمَكَرُواْ وَمَكَرَ أَللّه وَأَللّه خَيْرُ الْمَاكِرِينَ {أَل عمران/54}

The person should be in the full-red-alert state of the person with positive uncertainty. This station can be called tayaqquz.

Tayaqquz requires the embodiment of La Hawla wa la Quwwata illa Billah. There is no spiritual and physical power or enablement except the enablement of Allah ﷻ.

In this sense, the person relies on the One Who has the Qudrah and Full Power, Allah ﷻ.

Tayaqquz reminds the person that the spiritual red alert state of alertness with any makr of Allah ﷻ with tests or trials is a possibility. This person responds this possible extreme tension in spiritual state of the person formed with tayaqquz-alertness with La hawla wa la Quwwata

---

63. Then did they feel secure from the plan of Allah? But no one feels secure from the plan of Allah except the losing people.
64. And they planned, but Allah planned. And Allah is the best of planners.

illa Billah. Then, inshAllah the state of balance or middle way as Sirāt al-Mustaqīm is maintained with the Tawfīq, Fadl, and Karam of Allah ﷻ.

Here is a possible depiction of this critical spiritual state of the person:

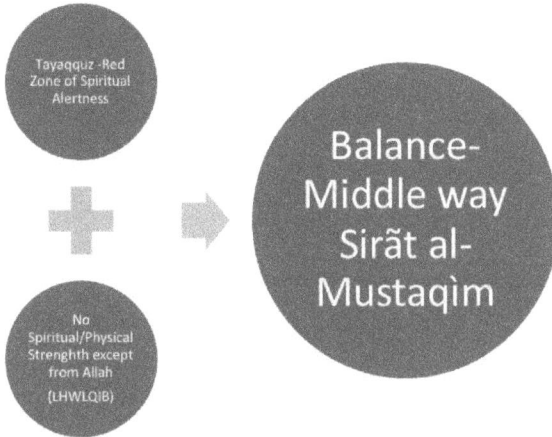

Tayaqquz -Red Zone of Spiritual Alertness

No Spiritual/Physical Strenghth except from Allah (LHWLQīB)

Balance-Middle way Sirāt al-Mustaqīm

This balance may not be easy for the person to constantly maintain. Yet, it is the set goal as a guideline or a pillar knowledge for the person to implement in true journey on the path of Allah ﷻ.

In this regard, the guidelines in spiritual journeys are super but super critical.

The person should not start this journey if he or she does not know the main guidelines.

It is better for this person stay as a minimalist as one day, a person came to the Prophet ﷺ and asked minimum external requirements of Islām to be in Jannah-Heaven [9]. Rasulullah ﷺ then informed him with the required pillars. After the man left, he ﷺ mentioned that if he is truthful in implementing these requirements, then he will be the man of Jannah-Heaven. There is nothing wrong to be minimalist. As we are all different, everyone is on a true journey as long as they know and use the main pillars of live vests when they dive into the ocean of knowledge and experience on the path of Allah ﷻ, al-Baki, the Infinite.

May Allah ﷻ protect us in this tough and difficult journey, Amìn. At any time, the person can slip, swallow and die but may not realize

الَّذِينَ ضَلَّ سَعْيُهُمْ فِي الْحَيَاةِ الدُّنْيَا وَهُمْ يَحْسَبُونَ أَنَّهُمْ يُحْسِنُونَ صُنْعًا mentioned[65] it as
[16 {104/الكهف}]

May Allah ﷻ make us follow with istiqamah-balance and continuity-Sirāt al-Mustaqìm-the middle way/balance pleasing Allah ﷻ on the path of Rasulullah ﷺ, Amìn.

أللهُمَّ صَلِّ على سيدنا محمد ﷺ وعلى آله وصحبه وسلم

Allahumma Salli ala Sayyidina Muhammad ﷺ wa a'lā ālihi wa sahbihi wa sallim.

Juz 13

Sûrah 13 al-R'ad

[13][66]

الَّذِينَ آمَنُواْ وَتَطْمَئِنُّ قُلُوبُهُم بِذِكْرِ اللّهِ أَلاَ بِذِكْرِ اللّهِ تَطْمَئِنُّ الْقُلُوبُ
{28/الرعد}

Bleeding Hearts & its Medicine

One should remember that the heart needs Allah ﷻ constantly.

Regardless of the person realizes or not, the heart is need of Allah ﷻ.

Regardless of the person makes sufficient remembering of Allah ﷻ, heart is need of Allah ﷻ. Regardless of the person, the person has imān or kufr, heart needs Allah ﷻ.

We constantly feel void, empty or sad. Even if this feeling comes for a second in the twenty four periods of a day, this feeling tells the person that heart needs Allah ﷻ.

If the person of imān, while thinking that he or she is in remembrance of Allah ﷻ yet, he or she feels the spiritual void, empty or sad emotions, then this person is not really in the remembrance of Allah ﷻ, Dhikrullah.

As a Muslim, sometimes we miss the tahajjud, a nawāfil or even fardh, this can put the person in a very disturbed states of feeling void, empty and sad. It is reported that when the sahabah (رضي الله عنهم) used to miss the beginning of an iqamah prayed in Jam'ah, they had the

---

65. [They are] those whose effort is lost in worldly life, while
they think that they are doing well in work."
66. Those who have believed and whose hearts are assured by the remembrance of Allah.
Unquestionably, by the remembrance of Allah hearts are assured."

utmost destructive feelings for three days that other sahabah used to visit him (رضي الله عنه), calming him (رضي الله عنه) and reminding him (رضي الله عنه) that Rahmah of Allah ﷻ is so vast that he should be easy on himself (رضي الله عنه).

In this case, one can see the sahabah's faculties of iman were fully awake and alert and they understood fully what they missed: a beginning of takbir in Jam'ah especially when it was led by the Rahmatan Lil-Alamìn ﷺ.

There are two problems here. One is that we don't realize our own problem. We take it easy. The other is even if we detect these feelings and state of our own selves and mind, we don't know how to address the problem.

The popular trends of overeating, snacking, hanging around and social media without any purpose are the ways that we try to address our problems by wrong means.

Our hearts are constantly bleeding and seeking for Allah ﷻ and the ways of Rasulullah ﷺ, al-Habìb ﷺ.

Yes, this life is a pain with all the possibilities of displeasing Allah ﷻ.

The pain of constant possibilities of displeasing Allah ﷻ can make this life for a genuine person of iman worst prison ever, even he or she seem to have the life of a king.

The pain of not being with Rasulullah ﷺ as a role model and as our imam ﷺ in front of us and witnessing all the Muslim in desperate conditions of scattered states can make this life for a genuine person of iman worst prison than ever.

Yet, Allah ﷻ is Merciful, ar-Rahmān ar-Rahìm. The Attribute of Allah ﷻ as ar-Rahmān ar-Rahìm constantly emphasized in the beginning of each Sûrah and twice in the opening of the Qurān in Sûrah Fatiha.

What does this tell us?

Yes, we need Allah ﷻ and Rasulullah ﷺ.

Yes, we have the reality of displeasing Allah ﷻ constantly in this life and this can put the person in the full shattered states of emptiness, voidness, grief in this life for the real person of iman.

Yes, we don't have Rasulullah ﷺ with us who can take us under his merciful wings ﷺ to protect us as the flies are going into the fire and Rasulullah ﷺ making a shield around the fire as mentioned in the hadith [10].

Those are realities.

Yet, Allah ﷻ is merficul as mentioned ar-Rahmãn ar-Rahìm.

Allah ﷻ left with us the Qurãn and Sunnah of Rasulullah ﷺ.

Therefore, allah ﷻ gave us the source of satisfaction for our hearts in this life with the Qurãn and sunnah of Rasulullah ﷺ.

أللهُمَّ جَعَلنَا مَن اتَّبِعُ سَبِيْلك و سبيل رَسُوْلك ﷺ

Allahumma Ja'alna man attabi'u sabilak wa sabili rasuluk ﷺ

أللهُمَّ صَلِّ عَلَى سَيِّدِنَا وَ حَبِيْبَنَا مُحَمّد ﷺ

Allahumma salli ala sayyidina wa habibina muhammad ﷺ.

Sorrow, Happiness, Purpose of Greed, Chaotic Hearts and Minds

الَّذِينَ آمَنُواْ وَتَطْمَئِنُّ قُلُوبُهُم بِذِكْرِ اللّهِ أَلاَ بِذِكْرِ اللّهِ تَطْمَئِنُّ الْقُلُوبُ

{الرعد/28}[67]

One should remember that when one remembers one's past engagements or the past, he or she can or can't detect the reasons of sorrow and happiness.

For the person of imãn, the reason of sorrow is the absence of ihsãn and Dhikrullah with sakina, tafakkur, tadabbur, tazzakur at that specific moment or many moments referred as past.

Yes, each moment of time that is void of ihsãn and true remembrance of Allah ﷻ as Dhikrullah, is the source of a melancholic pain in the person's heart and mind for the person of imãn.

Regardless of a person of imãn can detect this or not, this is the reality once the person tastes the sweetness of imãn, ihsãn, and Islãm.

For the people who are void of the true realities of imãn, Islãm and ihsãn, their source of happiness can be a pleasure of world. Their source of pain of grief and melancholy can be the absence and termination of this worldly pleasure.

Allah ﷻ gives us constant ni'mahs of air, food, water in our bodily sustenance. This is from the Fadl, Karam and Grace of Allah ﷻ. Allah ﷻ gives us as al-Wahhãb, al-Karìm, al-Hannãn, al-Mannan, al-Latìf. It is not because we deserve it.

---

67. Those who have believed and whose hearts are assured by the remembrance of Allah. Unquestionably, by the remembrance of Allah hearts are assured."

Similarly, Allah ﷻ gives us constant sakina and itminān, the true and real calmness, tranquility and satisfaction of the heart and mind spiritual sustenance called as Dhikrullah. This again is from the Fadl, Karam and Grace of Allah ﷻ. Allah ﷻ gives us as al-Wahhāb, al-Karìm, al-Hannān, al-Mannan, al-Latìf. It is not because we deserve it.

This is mentioned in the ayah as[68] الَّذِينَ آمَنُواْ وَتَطْمَئِنُّ قُلُوبُهُم بِذِكْرِ اِللَّه أَلَا بِذِكْرِ اللَّهِ تَطْمَئِنُّ الْقُلُوبُ {الرعد/28}

One of the Great Names of Allah ﷻ is al-Rahmān.

Allah ﷻ as al-Rahmān give all the physical needs of humans regardless of a kāfir or a mu'min. The Name of Allah ﷻ as al-Rahìm can indicate showering the blessings of Allah ﷻ especially for mu'min.

Similarly, the Name of Allah ﷻ as al-Rahman can allow all humans even if they are kāfir to receive some ingredients of a spiritual sustenance through silence, meditation, yoga, or other means of spiritual and engagements. Yet, these spiritual engagements of firāq dallah-deviated groups can just be a sample for them to really activate feeling of "greed" for full and true spiritual sustenance so that the seeker can look further and further for full and complete satisfaction, tranquility and calmness. So, it is not just a sample.

One can remember the case of Salman Fārisi (رضي الله عنه) as being first raised in a fire-worshipper household, then followed a Christian monk, then finalized his journey of searching with Islām, imān and ihsān. SubhanAllah!

Rasulullah ﷺ indicates this reality of the search for spiritual sustenance for the people of like Salman ra that if even this sustenance was at a very distant place, they would find it [17]. SubhanAllah!

A person of Islām, imān, and ihsān has the unending journey of satisfaction of sakina and itminān, tranquility, calmness and satisfaction of the heart and mind with Dhikrullah.

This ayah الَّذِينَ آمَنُواْ وَتَطْمَئِنُّ قُلُوبُهُم بِذِكْرِ اللَّهِ أَلاَ بِذِكْرِ اللَّهِ تَطْمَئِنُّ الْقُلُوبُ {الرعد/28} indicates this reality.

---

68. Those who have believed and whose hearts are assured by the remembrance of Allah. Unquestionably, by the remembrance of Allah hearts are assured."

On the path of Islām, imān and ihsān, there is no stop but non-ending increase and indulgence in ones connection with Allah ﷻ with Dhikrullah going spiritually further and further vertically.

Every feeling of a human being has its true usage and purpose.

Greed is present in humans to be not satisfied with Dhikrullah and Ma'rifatullah.

Dhikrullah and Ma'rifatullah are the sustenance of the heart and the mind.

One should remember our physical hearts are constantly in motion.

The constant physical motion of the heart with heartbeats can indicate the chaotic state of the spiritual heart without tranquility, sakina, calmness and itminān-satisfaction.

If our physical heart is similar to agitated crying babying, then Dhikrullah is its real pacifier. Or, in its true sense, Dhikrullah is similar to the milk that truly is a need for a suckling baby with all its vitamins, ingredients and benefits. SubhanAllah!

Dhikrullah is a similar to a mother's milk which is pure and beneficial.

The Primary Pure and Authentic Milk-Dhikrullah is the Qurān and Sunnah of Rasulullah ﷺ.

The constant neuro-signals occurring in the brain can indicate unending chaotic state of the mind with constant thinking or flow of thoughts without tranquility, sakina, calmness, and itminān-satisfaction.

If our physical brain is similar to the agitated a growing child constantly questioning everything for its purpose, then ma'rifatullah is its real answer. In its true sense, ma'rifatullah is the essential answer for a growing child or adults with a lot of questions for the purpose and meaning of their life. These true and real answer of these questions around ma'rifatullah is extremely critical to build one's life with a strong pillar compared to pillar of a house that is very weak similar to a spider as mentioned[69] مَثَلُ الَّذِينَ اتَّخَذُوا مِن دُونِ اللَّهِ أَوْلِيَاء كَمَثَلِ الْعَنكَبُوتِ اتَّخَذَتْ بَيْتًا وَإِنَّ وَأَوْهَنَ الْبُيُوتِ لَبَيْتُ الْعَنكَبُوتِ لَوْ كَانُوا يَعْلَمُونَ {العنكبوت/41}

SubhanAllah!

Ma'rifatullah is the essential purpose which is the real reality.

---

69. The example of those who take allies other than Allah is like that of the spider who takes a home. And indeed, the weakest of homes is the home of the spider, if they only knew.

The Primary Pure and Authentic Milk of Ma'rifatullah is wahiy, that is is the Qurān and Sunnah of Rasulullah ﷺ.

Our hearts and minds are constantly in chaotic states through the flow of emotions and thoughts.

Both emotions and thoughts should be regulated calmed and satisfied with Dhikrullah and Ma'rifatullah.

The daily engagements of five times prayers, Dhikrullah, recitation of the Qurān, all applications of sunnah of Rasulullah ﷺ, and our existence in this life with constant tafakkur, tadabbur and tazakkur all are the regulations to satisfy our hearts and minds.

The practice of awrād or wird are all systemized efforts to balance, regulate, calm and satisfy one's heart and mind.

May Allah ﷻ help us to achieve the state of Islām, Imān and Ihsān, Amìn.

أَللهُمَّ صَلِّ عَلَى سَيِّدِنَا وَ حَبِيْنَا مُحَمّد ﷺ

Allahumma Salli ala Sayyidina wa Habibina Muhammad, ﷺ

Diseases, Symptoms and Diagnosis

الَّذِينَ آمَنُواْ وَتَطْمَئِنُّ قُلُوبُهُم بِذِكْرِ اللهِ أَلاَ بِذِكْرِ اللهِ تَطْمَئِنُّ الْقُلُوبُ
{الرعد/28}

One should remember that Allah ﷻ is the only One to go constantly and relentlessly to go back with dua, istighfār, I'āna, help and protection.

One should remember our hearts are in the state of crying even if we realize or not.

When the tears reflect on our eyes, these can be realization points of the times that our hearts are crying.

Each crying with a tear is the representation of the crying of the heart.

At all times, the crying of the heart constantly tells the person that the heart yearns and desires to run to Allah ﷻ and calmed down and pacified with the remembrance of Allah ﷻ.

The ayah indicates this reality as mentioned[70] الَّذِينَ آمَنُواْ وَتَطْمَئِنُّ قُلُوبُهُم
بِذِكْرِ اللهِ أَلاَ بِذِكْرِ اللهِ تَطْمَئِنُّ الْقُلُوبُ {الرعد/28}

---

70. Those who have believed and whose hearts are assured by the remembrance of Allah. Unquestionably, by the remembrance of Allah hearts are assured."

The times of gaflah induced in us and constantly displayed as contraction of heart of stress, anxiety, fear, terror and panic. In all these times, our hearts cry and ask help and beg us to run Allah ﷻ.

Yet, when the person makes the habit of adapting and taking refuge in other things except Allah ﷻ, the heart deepens this state of anguish into the diseases with trauma.

In this case, arrogance is a representation of trauma of the heart. Jealousy is a representation of the trauma of the heart. Showing off-riyā is a representation of this trauma of the heart.

On the other hand, the display of trauma in outer sciences or externalities or diagnosis in legal terminologies can be shirk, kufr, and others.

If we take for example, analyze one trauma case of riyā-showing off with its process, below can be a possible representation.

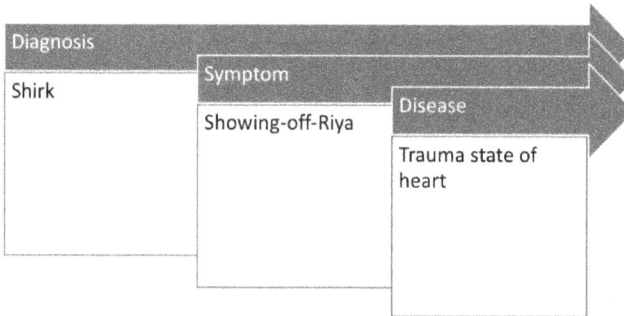

Diagnosis		
Shirk	Symptom	
	Showing-off-Riya	Disease
		Trauma state of heart

In the above diagram, traumatic disease of the heart displays its symptoms as showing-off riya. Then, its diagnosis in legal and official term becomes shirk.

In all engagements, there is no legal system of judging the people. Everyone is expected to establish their own self judiciary systems of judgments and prosecutions to take into oneself in self-accountability. At the end of the day, when the person dies, the Ultimate Judge, Allah ﷻ will reveal the person's fair or unfair judgments in this self-judiciary systems of courts only and truly known by the person and Allah ﷻ. This is mentioned as[71] {الحج/69} أَللهُ يَحْكُمُ بَيْنَكُمْ يَوْمَ الْقِيَامَةِ فِيمَا كُنْتُمْ فِيهِ تَخْتَلِفُونَ

Therefore, in Islām and all the books sent by Allah ﷻ in human common court systems everything is based on externalities of

---

71. Allah will judge between you on the Day of Resurrection concerning that over which you used to differ."

implementation of social justices. It is illegal in this law system as instructed by the scriptures (shariāh) to execute a person due to his or her intention, thought or emotions that were not displayed as an action harming others or the public.

On the other hand, the execution of the Judgment in front of Allah ﷻ in afterlife is primarily based on this self-judiciary system of judgment based on the person's real intention and thoughts known only by the person and Allah ﷻ.

May Allah ﷻ make us establish a fair and a self-court system taking our own selves in self-accountabilty that is pleased by Allah ﷻ following the path of Rasulullah ﷺ, Amīn.

أَللهُمَّ صَلِّ على سَيِّدنا مُحَمَّد وعلى آله سيدنا محمد كَمَا صَلَّيْتَ على سَيِّدنا إبراهيم وعلى آل سيدنا إبراهيم إنك حميد مجيد

Allahumma Salli A'la Sayyidina Muhammad wa a'la a'li Sayyidina Muhammad Kama Sallayta a'la Sayyidina Ibrāhim wa a'la Sayyidina Ibrāhim Innaka Hāmidun Majīd

[22-24]

Patience, the Goal and Results

وَالَّذِينَ صَبَرُواْ ابْتِغَاء وَجْهِ رَبِّهِمْ وَأَقَامُواْ الصَّلاَةَ وَأَنفَقُواْ مِمَّا رَزَقْنَاهُمْ سِرًّا وَعَلاَنِيَةً وَيَدْرَؤُونَ بِالْحَسَنَةِ السَّيِّئَةَ أُوْلَئِكَ لَهُمْ عُقْبَى الدَّارِ {22/الرعد}[72]

جَنَّاتُ عَدْنٍ يَدْخُلُونَهَا وَمَنْ صَلَحَ مِنْ آبَائِهِمْ وَأَزْوَاجِهِمْ وَذُرِّيَّاتِهِمْ وَالمَلاَئِكَةُ يَدْخُلُونَ عَلَيْهِم مِّن كُلِّ بَابٍ {23/الرعد}[73] سَلاَمٌ عَلَيْكُم بِمَا صَبَرْتُمْ فَنِعْمَ عُقْبَى الدَّارِ {24/الرعد}[74]

وَجَزَاهُم بِمَا صَبَرُوا جَنَّةً وَحَرِيرًا {12/الإنسان}[75]

---

72. And those who are patient, seeking the countenance of their Lord, and establish prayer and spend from what We have provided for them secretly and publicly and prevent evil with good - those will have the good consequence of [this] home -
73. Gardens of perpetual residence; they will enter them with whoever were righteous among their fathers, their spouses and their descendants. And the angels will enter upon them from every gate, [saying],
74. "Peace be upon you for what you patiently endured. And excellent is the final home."
75. And will reward them for what they patiently endured [with] a garden [in Paradise] and silk [garments].

يَا أَيُّهَا الَّذِينَ آمَنُواْ اصْبِرُواْ وَصَابِرُواْ وَرَابِطُواْ وَاتَّقُواْ اللَّهَ لَعَلَّكُمْ تُفْلِحُونَ
{آل عمران/200}[76]

وَأَطِيعُواْ اللَّهَ وَرَسُولَهُ وَلاَ تَنَازَعُواْ فَتَفْشَلُواْ وَتَذْهَبَ رِيحُكُمْ وَاصْبِرُواْ إِنَّ اللَّهَ مَعَ الصَّابِرِينَ
{{الأنفال/46}[77]

وَاسْتَعِينُواْ بِالصَّبْرِ وَالصَّلاَةِ وَإِنَّهَا لَكَبِيرَةٌ إِلاَّ عَلَى الْخَاشِعِينَ
{البقرة/45}[78]

One should know that the trait of patience can be sufficient for the person to handle most of the problems in life. With patience, the person can be successful in this life and afterlife.

Yet, there are factors that run against the maintenance of patience in the person.

The first one is that the person thinks that this life will not end and therefore, he or she should move on in decision making not to "ruin" rest of his or her life. Yet, this decision making performed with haste can actually ruin rest of one's short remaining life as mentioned[79] وَأَطِيعُواْ اللَّهَ وَرَسُولَهُ وَلاَ تَنَازَعُواْ فَتَفْشَلُواْ وَتَذْهَبَ رِيحُكُمْ وَاصْبِرُواْ إِنَّ اللَّهَ مَعَ الصَّابِرِينَ {الأنفال/46}

In other words, if the person knows that this life is short, temporary and a place of transit but not a real place of residence as mentioned many places in the Qurān and sunnah of Rasulullah ﷺ, then the person really may not give much value for the effects of immediate, instant and temporal incidents.

He or she should shape all one's engagement, planning and decision making around this critical perspective that "I am here few more time either as days, seconds or years. Therefore, let me don't waste my time with people's attitudes, tantrums, and ill-treatments and move forward in preparation for my akhirah."

Yet, it is very difficult to be not affected for the lowly people like us making small things as a big deal in family, social and professional

---

76. O you who have believed, persevere and endure and remain stationed and fear Allah that you may be successful.
77. And obey Allah and His Messenger, and do not dispute and [thus] lose courage and [then] your strength would depart; and be patient. Indeed, Allah is with the patient.
78. And seek help through patience and prayer, and indeed, it is difficult except for the humbly submissive [to Allah]
79. And obey Allah and His Messenger, and do not dispute and [thus] lose courage and [then] your strength would depart; and be patient. Indeed, Allah is with the patient.

life without any patience as mentioned with وَإِنَّهَا لَكَبِيرَةٌ in وَاسْتَعِينُواْ بِالصَّبْرِ
وَالصَّلاَةِ وَإِنَّهَا لَكَبِيرَةٌ إِلاَّ عَلَى الْخَاشِعِينَ {البقرة/45}[80]

When one reviews the life of Rasulullah ﷺ, he ﷺ was always goal oriented but not swayed around with the effects of incidents that one can easily lose his or her patience.

In these incidents, either he ﷺ smiled, or most of the time, he ﷺ kept silence with patience. In most of the incidents, he ﷺ very gently and kindly corrected and addressed the issue if it entails the right of people and Allah ﷻ. In some cases, he ﷺ addressed it directly in a very gentle and caring way, and sometimes, he addressed the problem and issue in a general address of khutbah-sermon.

Yet, most of the time, due to his embodiment of his character ﷺ in his actions ﷺ, he ﷺ did not engage in the verbal correction of the matter. The people corrected themselves by observing and approximating the meanings of his expectations ﷺ.

Therefore, he was Rasulullah ﷺ, al-Habīb ﷺ.

The ones who followed his path as the awliyaullah, they took similar approaches.

One of them said [18] "if I see people are in the fire dying and I am running to save them, and at this rush, if people bumped into me, I don't have time or interest to deal with them." Similarly, "the people are dying without imān similar to dying in fire. My goal is to help and save them. I don't have time with other distractions even people hurt me." SubhanAllah!

This was the reflection of the approach of Rasulullah ﷺ on one of the awliyaullah and one can find similar life perspectives in the lives of other awliyaullah today and in the past.

One should remember that we should be extremely careful not to dissolve ourselves in petty and instant things.

We have a very high goal that is to please Allah ﷻ.

At the times of losing our patience, one should constantly remind oneself this high goal and ask if losing one's patience, acting accordingly and making a decision would serve this high goal or it is going to displease Allah ﷻ.

SubhanAllah!

---

80. And seek help through patience and prayer, and indeed, it is difficult except for the humbly submissive [to Allah]

وَالَّذِينَ صَبَرُواْ ابْتِغَاء وَجْهِ رَبِّهِمْ وَأَقَامُواْ الصَّلاَةَ وَأَنفَقُواْ مِمَّا   This is mentioned as
رَزَقْنَاهُمْ سِرًّا وَعَلاَنِيَةً وَيَدْرَؤُونَ بِالْحَسَنَةِ السَّيِّئَةَ أُوْلَئِكَ لَهُمْ عُقْبَى الدَّارِ {الرعد/22}[81]

May Allah 🕮 help us!

The matter is so serious.

Yet, we are stuck constantly on the roadblocks of our own nafs preventing us being patient and to go forward in order to please Allah 🕮.

أَللهُمَّ صَلِّ عَلَى سَيِّدِنَا وَ حَبِيْبِنَا مُحَمَّد 🕮

Allahumma Salli ala Sayyidina wa Habibina Muhammad 🕮

أَللهُمَّ صَلِّ على سَيِّدَنا مُحَمَّد وعلى آله سيدنا محمد كَمَا صَلَّيْتَ على سَيِّدنا إبراهيم وعلى آل سيدنا إبراهيم إنك حميد مجيد

Allahumma Salli ala Sayyidina Muhammad wa a'la āli Sayyidina Muhammad 🕮 kama sallayte a'la Sayyidina Ibrāhim wa a'la āli Sayyidina Ibrāhim Innaka Hamidun Majìd.

Juz 14

Sûrah 15 al-Hijr

[24][82]

Exchange of Levels, Everyone as a Potential Waliyullah, & Gentleness in Uslûb

وَلَقَدْ عَلِمْنَا الْمُسْتَقْدِمِينَ مِنكُمْ وَلَقَدْ عَلِمْنَا الْمُسْتَأْخِرِينَ
{الحجر/24}

One should remember Allah 🕮 is al-Qādir. We constantly need Allah 🕮 in our all engagements, thoughts, emotions, and actions.

Anything or anyone can affect the person in a negative way and induce some feelings in the person's rûh-soul and heart.

Sometimes, a word, an email, a text or a look can disturb the person although the person knows the answer and solution to the effects of these external agents.

---

81. And those who are patient, seeking the countenance of their Lord, and establish prayer and spend from what We have provided for them secretly and publicly and prevent evil with good—those will have the good consequence of [this] home -
82. And We have already known the preceding [generations] among you, and We have already known the later [ones to come].

At any time, one should not forget his or her constant dependency on Allah ﷻ. If Allah ﷻ does not give the strength, hawl and quwwah, the person cannot really handle a simple looking or a piece of cake-looking incident. The full embodiment of faqr and ajz-spiritual poverty and weakness is required in front of Rabbul Alamin ﷻ. The state of faqr and ajz is not embodied for people but only only for Allah ﷻ.

Yet, the embodiment of this state in front of Allah ﷻ can also balance and modulate our actions how we solve and address the problems with humans and all creation.

Being full dependency on Allah ﷻ with faqr and ajz requires gentleness, care and kindness in our interactions with humans and all creation. At any time, Allah ﷻ can replace the positions and switch the levels as mentioned[83] .وَلَقَدْ عَلِمْنَا الْمُسْتَقْدِمِينَ مِنكُمْ وَلَقَدْ عَلِمْنَا الْمُسْتَأْخِرِينَ {24/ الحجر} May Allah ﷻ protect us from the bad endings, Amìn.

On the other hand, some can think that being full dependency on Allah ﷻ with faqr and ajz can make the person harsher in relationships with others because a person can deduce that since he is now fully dependent on Allah ﷻ, he is on the right path, therefore, he has a higher status than others and therefore, they need an attitude of firmness reflecting with harshness while interacting with others because now, the person is not dependent on except Allah ﷻ.

One should realize that the first part of above statement is true as that when a person is fully dependent on Allah ﷻ, then inshAllah he or she can be on the right path.

Yet, no one has certainty that he or she would keep that state. At any time, Allah ﷻ can swap and exchange the people with their levels and status with a hikmah-wisdom and due to free-will ingredients of the deliberate inclinations of the individual.

There are a lot of examples of this. Shaytān is the prime example due to his wrong feelings of security and superiority with the assumption that he is dependent on Allah ﷻ, and he is on the right path, therefore he has a higher status, therefore, he had a judgement call of harshness or firmness towards humans indicating arrogance on this part. Then, the levels with a hikmah-wisdom and due to free will choice of Shaytān is all swapped. Shaytān went to the lowest of low and humans in the leadership

---

83. And We have already known the preceding [generations] among you, and We have already known the later [ones to come].

of Rasulullah ﷺ went to highest of the high in their relationship with
Allah ﷻ. May Allah ﷻ protect us, Amìn.

قَالَ يَا إِبْلِيسُ مَا مَنَعَكَ أَن تَسْجُدَ لِمَا خَلَقْتُ بِيَدَيَّ أَسْتَكْبَرْتَ أَمْ
كُنتَ مِنَ الْعَالِينَ {57/ص} قَالَ أَنَا خَيْرٌ مِّنْهُ خَلَقْتَنِي مِن نَّارٍ وَخَلَقْتَهُ مِن طِينٍ {76/ص}
قَالَ فَاخْرُجْ مِنْهَا فَإِنَّكَ رَجِيمٌ {77/ص} وَإِنَّ عَلَيْكَ لَعْنَتِي إِلَى يَوْمِ الدِّينِ {78/ص} قَالَ رَبِّ
فَأَنظِرْنِي إِلَى يَوْمِ يُبْعَثُونَ {79/ص} قَالَ فَإِنَّكَ مِنَ الْمُنظَرِينَ {80/ص} إِلَى يَوْمِ الْوَقْتِ الْمَعْلُومِ
{81/ص} قَالَ فَبِعِزَّتِكَ لَأُغْوِيَنَّهُمْ أَجْمَعِينَ {82/ص} إِلَّا عِبَادَكَ مِنْهُمُ الْمُخْلَصِينَ {83/ص}

Shaytān did not realize his explicit uslûp of the judgment call and
went further and further with hate, jealousy and revenge as mentioned
قَالَ فَبِعِزَّتِكَ لَأُغْوِيَنَّهُمْ أَجْمَعِينَ {82/ص}. May Allah ﷻ protect us, Amìn!

It is important to catch our judgment calls before it turns to
irreversible states of hate, jealousy and revenge similar to Shaytān. May
Allah ﷻ protect us, Amìn!

The key element here is seeing everyone as the potential person of
ahlullah that Allah ﷻ can raise the level of that person and lower my or
your status due to our intrinsic or extrinsic free-will ingredients of the
deliberate inclinations of the individual with judgment and arrogance.
May Allah ﷻ protect us, Amìn.

Understanding this critical element can transform one's actions in
uslûb-methodology to the excellent manners of gentleness, care, and
kindness. May Allah ﷻ makes us from them, Amìn.

Rasulullah ﷺ had the highest understanding and embodiment of
this reality as mentioned[85] {107/الأنبياء} وَمَا أَرْسَلْنَاكَ إِلَّا رَحْمَةً لِّلْعَالَمِينَ

Therefore, Rasulullah ﷺ had the highest level of gentle, care,
Rahmah, and kindness for everyone and everything.

Therefore, Rasulullah ﷺ had the success with the Grace and Tawfìq
of Allah ﷻ people gathering around him with awe, astonishment and
following his pearl and diamond style and uslûb sweeter than honey ﷺ.

---

84. [38:75] [Allah] said, "O Iblees, what prevented you from prostrating to that which I created
with My hands? Were you arrogant [then], or were you [already] among the haughty?" [38:76]
He said, "I am better than him. You created me from fire and created him from clay." [38:77]
[Allah] said, "Then get out of Paradise, for indeed, you are expelled. [38:78] And indeed, upon
you is My curse until the Day of Recompense." [38:79] He said, "My Lord, then reprieve me
until the Day they are resurrected." [38:80] [Allah] said, "So indeed, you are of those reprieved
[38:81] Until the Day of the time well-known." [38:82] [Iblees] said, "By your might, I will surely
mislead them all [38:83] Except, among them, Your chosen servants."
85. And We have not sent you, [O Muhammad], except as a mercy to the worlds.

فَبِمَا رَحْمَةٍ مِّنَ اللهِ لِنتَ لَهُمْ وَلَوْ كُنتَ فَظًّا غَلِيظَ الْقَلْبِ ⁸⁶This is mentioned as لَانفَضُّواْ مِنْ حَوْلِكَ فَاعْفُ عَنْهُمْ وَاسْتَغْفِرْ لَهُمْ وَشَاوِرْهُمْ فِي الْأَمْرِ فَإِذَا عَزَمْتَ فَتَوَكَّلْ عَلَى اللهِ إِنَّ اللهَ يُحِبُّ الْمُتَوَكِّلِينَ {آل عمران/159} إِن يَنصُرْكُمُ اللهُ فَلَا غَالِبَ لَكُمْ وَإِن يَخْذُلْكُمْ فَمَن ذَا الَّذِي يَنصُرُكُم مِّن بَعْدِهِ وَعَلَى اللهِ فَلْيَتَوَكَّلِ الْمُؤْمِنُونَ {آل عمران/160}

In the above ayahs, Allah ﷻ emphasizes tawakkul and only being dependent on Allah ﷻ as mentioned إِن يَنصُرْكُمُ اللهُ فَلَا غَالِبَ لَكُمْ وَإِن يَخْذُلْكُمْ . Yet, at the فَمَن ذَا الَّذِي يَنصُرُكُم مِّن بَعْدِهِ وَعَلَى اللهِ فَلْيَتَوَكَّلِ الْمُؤْمِنُونَ {آل عمران/160} same time, keeping the uslûb of gentleness, softness and kindness as Rasulullah ﷺ embodied as mentioned فَبِمَا رَحْمَةٍ مِّنَ اللهِ لِنتَ لَهُمْ وَلَوْ كُنتَ فَظًّا غَلِيظَ الْقَلْبِ لَانفَضُّواْ مِنْ حَوْلِكَ فَاعْفُ عَنْهُمْ وَاسْتَغْفِرْ لَهُمْ وَشَاوِرْهُمْ فِي الْأَمْرِ فَإِذَا عَزَمْتَ فَتَوَكَّلْ عَلَى اللهِ إِنَّ اللهَ يُحِبُّ الْمُتَوَكِّلِينَ {آل عمران/159}.

Realization of these realities and acting on these realities with ikhlās is only with the Rahmah and Tawfiq of Allah ﷻ as mentioned فَبِمَا رَحْمَةٍ مِّنَ اللهِ لِنتَ لَهُمْ. Therefore, one should ask from Allah ﷻ constantly these states, actions, attitudes, uslûb and embodiment. May Allah ﷻ follow the path of Rasulullah ﷺ al Habib ﷺ in being layyin and in having tawakkul on Allah ﷻ, Amîn. Allahumma Salli ala Sayyidina Muhammad ﷺ.

There were many incidents that Rasulullah ﷺ reminded this reality to the Sahabah with their intrinsic realities not known by people, SubhanAllah!

A woman under the punishment due to zina and a judgment call against her appears, then Rasulullah ﷺ immediately reminds the reality of her high state in her tawbah [19] and her high status with Allah ﷻ. A man involved in some major sins and Rasulullah ﷺ reminds the people about his unknown very high status as that he loves Allah ﷻ and Rasulullah 19] ﷺ].

Yes, everything is due to our judgment calls. That is our problem!

Then, this affects our actions about how we talk to people, how we treat them with harshness, and with the feelings of superiority, shouting, not listening and then claiming that we are arguing and struggling for the sake of Allah ﷻ!

What a Shame!

---

86. **[3:159]** So by mercy from Allah, [O Muhammad], you were lenient with them. And if you had been rude [in speech] and harsh in heart, they would have disbanded from about you. So pardon them and ask forgiveness for them and consult them in the matter. And when you have decided, then rely upon Allah. Indeed, Allah loves those who rely [upon Him] **[3:160]** If Allah should aid you, no one can overcome you; but if He should forsake you, who is there that can aid you after Him? And upon Allah let the believers rely.

How many people we destroyed in our deliberate engagements on the path of religion!

How many times we destroyed ourselves by destroying others as "every action has a reaction!"

May Allah ﷻ protect us, Amìn!

The responsibility is so delicate, needs care, gentleness, and kindness.

Rasulullah ﷺ embodied this rûh-soul. We need to really revive the [87]Muhammadian ﷺ Rûh-Soul to give ourselves a life again with the Grace, Fadl and Rahmah of Allah ﷻ.

If we don't, then people will disappear, and we will disappear with them due to our harshness and coarse treatments on the path.

May Allah ﷻ protect us, Amìn!

May Allah ﷻ make us follow the path of gentleness, care, judgement free attitude and kindness in our uslûb-ways of talking, acting, thinking and writing, Amìn!

May Allah ﷻ make us follow the Ultimate Pearl and Diamond ﷺ , al-Mustafa ﷺ al-Habìb ﷺ, Amìn!

أَللهُمَّ صَلِّ عَلَى سَيِّدِنَا وَ حَبِيْبَنَا مُحَمّد ﷺ ،المُصطفى ﷺ

Allahumma Salli Ala Sayyidina wa Habibina Muhammad ﷺ, al Mustafa ﷺ.

Juz 15

Sûrah 18 Al-Kahf

[39][88]

Being Lost On the Path of Allah ﷻ without any Strength

وَلَوْ لَا إِذْ دَخَلْتَ جَنَّتَكَ قُلْتَ مَا شَاء اللهُ لَا قُوَّةَ إِلَّا بِاللَّهِ إِن تُرَنِ أَنَا أَقَلَّ مِنكَ مَالًا وَوَلَدًا }
39/الكهف}

One should know that we are weak and we need Allah ﷻ in our lives constantly. Our means and efforts of connecting ourselves with the

---

87. Although this term may not be so respectful for Rasulullah ﷺ, and I don't prefer to use it, this is used here as an exception.

88. And why did you, when you entered your garden, not say, 'What Allah willed [has occurred]; there is no power except in Allah '? Although you see me less than you in wealth and children,

recitation of the Qurān, salāh, dua, or any type of Dhikrullah can give the person power of purpose and goal to live and continue in this life journey.

Therefore, if one feels utmost weakness in their willpower of not able to lift even his or her finger, then he or she should push all his or her efforts to remember Allah ﷻ and to perform Dhikrullah ﷻ.

One can remember the narrations about the serial killer who were looking for repentance as mentioned in the hadith by Rasulullah [10] ﷺ 9]]. He was going to different places to ask advice from people. When the time of death came while he was dying he pushed himself to the place where he was looking for guidance for turning to Allah ﷻ and asking forgiveness from Allah ﷻ.

Our hearts constantly seek for Allah ﷻ. Sometimes, the overwhelming preoccupation of good-seeming things can make us lose our balance in our relationship with Allah ﷻ and our purpose and goal in life. At these times, before something breaks us such as an evil-seeming incident, we should maximize our all effort to break the chains around us to remember our real goal and purpose around the sweetness of imān and connection with Allah ﷻ with Dhikrullah.

If a person becomes stressed and cannot connect to the sweetness of imān through Dhikrullah, then this person may be in loss even though he or she may seem to be doing something virtuous and good.

One should always remember to activate the power of dua at all times and at this time. Dua is turning to Allah ﷻ to ask help and transformation should be always the life vest of the person. Dua to Allah ﷻ is the activation of the power of a person.

May Allah ﷻ protect us in our short life with useless engagements, thoughts, and thinking that we are pleasing Allah ﷻ but Allah ﷻ is not pleased with us.

May Allah ﷻ gives us the mayl-inclination, intention, willpower-irādah, and qudrah-power to make dua and to be constantly with Allah ﷻ with Dhikrullah in ihsān and at the same, trying our utmost effort to help others, Amìn.

اَللّٰهُمَّ صَلِّ عَلَى سَيِّدِنَا وَ حَبِيْبِنَا مُحَمَّد ﷺ،

Allahumma Salli a'la Sayyidina wa Habìbina Muhammad ﷺ.

Juz 17

Sûrah 21 al-Anbiyā

[83]⁸⁹

Spiritual Injuries & Hate of Dhikrullah

وَأَيُّوبَ إِذْ نَادَى رَبَّهُ أَنِّي مَسَّنِيَ الضُّرُّ وَأَنتَ أَرْحَمُ الرَّاحِمِينَ

{الأنبياء/83}

One should remember that there is a relationship with sins, spiritual injuries such as skepticism, imān and pleasure from Dhikrullah as the rûh-soul of the person demands and seeks for.

This relationship is depicted as

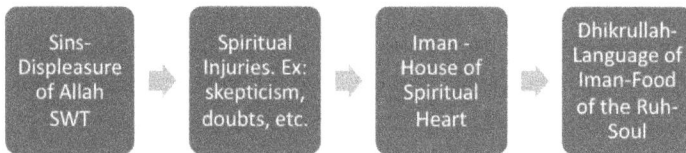

Yes, each sin represents the displeasure of Allah ﷻ causing a spiritual injury in one's heart. This spiritual injury can be a doubt, and bleeding wounds of skepticism on the heart, the place of imān. Then, spiritual heart starts bleeding where it holds and houses the imān.

One should remember that the language of imān is Dhikrullah. When the house of imān, the spiritual heart is bleeding, then the imān of the person is affected and then the language of imān, Dhikrullah is affected.

One should remember that a person of spiritual injury distances oneself from imān.

Accordingly, this person distances oneself from Dhikrullah.

In other words, a person of spiritual injury distances oneself from Dhikrullah with hate.

This is often due to sins and engagements of the person with the displeasure of Allah ﷻ causing spiritual injury.

---

89. And [mention] Job, when he called to his Lord, "Indeed, adversity has touched me, and you are the Most Merciful of the merciful."

One can find a lot of examples of an engagement of a person with Dhikrullah in a group that the person can be in ease and taking pleasure from Dhikrullah with this engagement.

On the other hand, when the person is alone, this may be difficult.

This can be due to the reality that the person still has some type of spiritual injury preventing him or her in solo engagement. Yet, in a group engagement, the extra empowerment of Allah ﷻ given on Jam'ah or group moves the person along similar to running falls or river when the person jumps in, then the person goes with the flow.

Therefore, sometimes, when the person is especially imbedded in personal sins of disconnect with Dhikrullah, then group engagements can help him or her to give an impulse or some type of ignition to recharge and reactivate the spiritual battery.

One should remember that Dhikrullah is a general term used to indicate the remembrance of Allah ﷻ with action, language, and thoughts. Dhikrullah can be memorization, recitation and analysis of the Qurān, analysis and implementation of sunnah of Rasulullah ﷺ, or it can be any good action and statement as Khayr on the path of Allah ﷻ and Rasulullah ﷺ.

It is mentioned that in the story of Ayyub (عليه السلام) when the trial and tribulation affected the place of his Dhikrullah, Ayyub (عليه السلام) made dua to Allah ﷻ to remove this tribulation and Allah ﷻ answered his dua and removed it from him [18]. This is indicated as[90] وَأَيُّوبَ إِذْ نَادَى

رَبَّهُ أَنِّي مَسَّنِيَ الضُّرُّ وَأَنتَ أَرْحَمُ الرَّاحِمِينَ {الأنبياء/38}

Similarly, we should constantly and at all times make dua to Allah ﷻ for the removal of our spiritual injuries causing alienation and estrangement from Dhikrullah.

May Allah ﷻ protect us from the sins and all the actions, thoughts, and statements leading to Displeasure of Allah ﷻ Amìn.

May Allah ﷻ make us follow the path of Allah ﷻ and Rasulullah ﷺ alone and together in a group/Jamah, Amìn.

أَللّهُمَّ صَلِّ عَلَى سَيِّدِنَا وَ حَبِيْبِنَا مُحَمّد ﷺ

Allahumma Salli Sayyidina wa Habibina Muhammad ﷺ.

---

90. And [mention] Job, when he called to his Lord, "Indeed, adversity has touched me, and you are the Most Merciful of the merciful."

[87]

The Realities of Problems & The Absence of Fake Help

وَذَا النُّونِ إِذ ذَّهَبَ مُغَاضِبًا فَظَنَّ أَن لَّن نَّقْدِرَ عَلَيْهِ فَنَادَى فِي الظُّلُمَاتِ أَن لَّا إِلَهَ إِلَّا أَنتَ سُبْحَانَكَ إِنِّي كُنتُ مِنَ الظَّالِمِينَ
{الأنبياء/87}

One should remember that our needs are countless. When we remember our physical, emotional and mental needs, they all get affected with different engagements at all times.

One should always self-evaluate the harm and benefit of each engagement with a critical risk analysis affecting our emotions, body, heart and mind.

If we consider the current situation of humanity in all countries with oppression and abuse at group and individual levels, then the person gets really affected.

If we consider the current situation of groups such as the women, children and other ethnic groups being abused and oppressed and killed, then the person gets really affected.

If we consider the current situation of these problems among Muslim and Muslim countries with the above problems, then the person gets really affected and shattered further especially when and if some people even justify their action by using the religious teachings. May Allah ﷻ protect us, Amìn.

If we witness about the people who have Muslims family members in their families, but they themselves are not Muslims because the father or Muslim care giver was not able to teach Islām to them and they grew up in a society with the crowd of non-Muslims with the absence of Islām, then the person gets really affected.

If we witness people who are raised in Muslim households but now isolated themselves from them and blaming themselves about their problems due to their upbringing with religious education, then the person gets really affected.

If we consider the current situation of the people and individuals without imān, dying in chaos and darkness with the trends of depression, committing suicide and other problems, then the person gets really affected.

Those are all realities and they are happening as we read and write these lines.

Yet knowing, remembering and realizing that:

► Allah ﷻ is in charge of everything.

► Allah ﷻ can change anything at any time.

► Allah ﷻ do not look neither the worldly or religious achievements but our individual efforts by ourselves individually and in a group/Jam'ah if we are doing something together.

We should remember that sometimes, the reasonable realities of means of help and apparent evidents can block us to connect ourselves with Allah ﷻ.

When we witness today, the absence of reasons, means, and powers to seek help from, except Allah ﷻ, then this can make the person vertically excel in one's relationship with Allah ﷻ. Because, there is no apparent means to seek help except Allah ﷻ. Alhamdulillah!

Now, everything becomes crystal clear! One can see the Real Cause behind all fake ones.

When we remember the dua of Yunus alayhi salam لَّا إِلَهَ إِلَّا أَنتَ سُبْحَانَكَ وَذَا النُّونِ إِذ ذَّهَبَ مُغَاضِبًا فَظَنَّ أَن لَّن نَّقْدِرَ عَلَيْهِ as mentioned إِنِّي كُنتُ مِنَ الظَّالِمِينَ this, فَنَادَى فِي الظُّلُمَاتِ أَن لَّا إِلَهَ إِلَّا أَنتَ سُبْحَانَكَ إِنِّي كُنتُ مِنَ الظَّالِمِينَ {87/الأنبياء} [91] is the reality.

There was no apparent reason, mean and power that was able to help Yunus alayhi salam except Allah ﷻ.

These are the times with all times that we need to turn to Allah ﷻ.

Yes, it is important that we don't get distracted and discouraged with the pessimistic worldview of the news, events, and actuality. Yet, we happen to hear it and when we sometimes happen to engage in chats, blurting with these devastating problems, one should always turn and run to Allah ﷻ for help and for istighfār in case the person involved his or her mind with something unnecessary distracting for that time and context.

May Allah ﷻ do not leave us with our own selves, Amìn

---

91. And [mention] the man of the fish, when he went off in anger and thought that We would not decree [anything] upon him. And he called out within the darknesses, "There is no deity except You; exalted are You. Indeed, I have been of the wrongdoers."

May Allah ❀ do not put us in the killing states of depression, pessimism, Amìn

May Allah ❀ transform of all our helplessness to the Divine Power, Qudrah following the path of the Qurān and Sunnah of Rasulullah ❀, Amìn.

أَللهُمَّ صَلِّ عَلَى سَيِّدِنَا وَ حَبِيْبِنَا مُحَمَّد ﷺ

Allahumma Salli ala Sayyidina wa Habibina Muhammad ❀.

[83-90]⁹²

Our Endless Needs & Names and Attributes of Allah ❀

وَأَيُّوبَ إِذْ نَادَى رَبَّهُ أَنِّي مَسَّنِيَ الضُّرُّ وَأَنتَ أَرْحَمُ الرَّاحِمِينَ {الأنبياء/83} فَاسْتَجَبْنَا لَهُ فَكَشَفْنَا مَا بِهِ مِن ضُرٍّ وَآتَيْنَاهُ أَهْلَهُ وَمِثْلَهُم مَّعَهُمْ رَحْمَةً مِّنْ عِندِنَا وَذِكْرَى لِلْعَابِدِينَ {الأنبياء/84}

وَذَا النُّونِ إِذ ذَّهَبَ مُغَاضِبًا فَظَنَّ أَن لَّن نَّقْدِرَ عَلَيْهِ فَنَادَى فِي الظُّلُمَاتِ أَن لَّا إِلَهَ إِلَّا أَنتَ سُبْحَانَكَ إِنِّي كُنتُ مِنَ الظَّالِمِينَ {الأنبياء/87} فَاسْتَجَبْنَا لَهُ وَنَجَّيْنَاهُ مِنَ الْغَمِّ وَكَذَلِكَ نُنجِي الْمُؤْمِنِينَ {الأنبياء/88}

وَزَكَرِيَّا إِذْ نَادَى رَبَّهُ رَبِّ لَا تَذَرْنِي فَرْدًا وَأَنتَ خَيْرُ الْوَارِثِينَ {الأنبياء/89} فَاسْتَجَبْنَا لَهُ وَوَهَبْنَا لَهُ يَحْيَى وَأَصْلَحْنَا لَهُ زَوْجَهُ إِنَّهُمْ كَانُوا يُسَارِعُونَ فِي الْخَيْرَاتِ وَيَدْعُونَنَا رَغَبًا وَرَهَبًا وَكَانُوا لَنَا خَاشِعِينَ {الأنبياء/90}

---

92. **[21:83]** And [mention] Job, when he called to his Lord, "Indeed, adversity has touched me, and you are the Most Merciful of the merciful." **[21:84]** So We responded to him and removed what afflicted him of adversity. And We gave him [back] his family and the like thereof with them as mercy from Us and a reminder for the worshippers [of Allah]. **[21:85]** And [mention] Ishmael and Idrees and Dhul-Kifl; all were of the patient. **[21:86]** And We admitted them into Our mercy. Indeed, they were of the righteous. **[21:87]** And [mention] the man of the fish, when he went off in anger and thought that We would not decree [anything] upon him. And he called out within the darknesses, "There is no deity except You; exalted are You. Indeed, I have been of the wrongdoers." **[21:88]** So We responded to him and saved him from the distress. And thus do We save the believers. **[21:89]** And [mention] Zechariah, when he called to his Lord, "My Lord, do not leave me alone [with no heir], while you are the best of inheritors." **[21:90]** So We responded to him, and We gave to him John, and amended for him his wife. Indeed, they used to hasten to good deeds and supplicate Us in hope and fear, and they were to Us humbly submissive.

One should know that Allah ﷻ placed in humans endless needs so that he or she can realize, turn and ask for the Divine Endless Rahmah, Grace, Fadl, Qudrah and Power.

If the person does not need something, then he or she does not realize an obvious reality. If he or she doesn't realize, the person does not learn and apply the teachings of this reality.

A human has endless intrinsic spiritual and physical faculties that lead the person in different endless grief, terror and stress states.

At the same time, a human has the potential of endless intrinsic spiritual and physical faculties that lead the person in different endless states of joy, happiness and calmness.

One should remember that humans have the potential collective seed of the different Attributes of Allah ﷻ in oneself. In this regard, a human is a sample of small or micro universe representing different Names and Attributes of Allah ﷻ.

In this regard, each need of the person that is a potential source of grief, sadness and stress serve for the purpose of the person turning to Allah ﷻ with dua with that specific Attribute/Name or Names of Allah ﷻ. If the person realizes this need, then he or she can look for solutions. The primary solution is to recognize that Allah ﷻ as being al-Rahmān and al-Rahìm can fulfill this need of the person especially with a specific Attribute and Name of Allah ﷻ addressing that person's need.

Therefore, if a person wakes up in a day, each day can bring a different manifestation of the Name and Attribute of Allah ﷻ in one's life. The alarm clock of this manifestation can be a feeling, emotion, thought, sadness, grief, stress seeking for that Name and Attribute of Allah ﷻ to relieve oneself in order to turn to Allah ﷻ with that specific Name and Attribute. Yet, Allah ﷻ is always al-Rahman and al-Rahìm.

In other words, the needs of a person coupled with alternating feelings in each second, minute, hour or day calls for Allah ﷻ with a specific Name and Attribute of Allah ﷻ.

A person should normalize this each day and night but not feel horrible and pessimistic but turn to Allah ﷻ with humbleness, humility seeking fulfilment of this need with a specific Name and Attribute of Allah ﷻ.

In this research of realization of this Name and Attribute of Allah ﷻ, observing the nature as the applied manifested Names and Attributes of Allah ﷻ is very critical.

In other words, nature is a laboratory of the Names and Attributes of Allah ﷻ to observe, discover, make synthesis and analysis. Then, one can take that Name and Attribute in one's life to fulfill one's needs by turning Fully to Allah ﷻ with that Name and Attribute of Allah ﷻ.

In all cases, regardless of the person have access spiritually, mentally, and emotionally to this laboratory, La ilaha illa Allah is the always general fulfilling Reality representing all the Names and Attributes of Allah ﷻ for the person of imān.

When the person embodies the realization of a specific Name and Attribute of Allah ﷻ, then at that time, the person dissolves one's self-ego with full humbleness, humility and debilitation of their limited power with full faqr and a'jz, then opens their hands, and turns to Allah ﷻ. Then, for sure, this is the time of display with certainty of the acceptance of one's dua due to turning to Allah ﷻ with their needs.

We can realize these examples in the dua of Yunus(عليه السلام) and Ayyub (عليه السلام) with full realization as:[93]

وَأَيُّوبَ إِذْ نَادَى رَبَّهُ أَنِّي مَسَّنِيَ الضُّرُّ وَأَنتَ أَرْحَمُ الرَّاحِمِينَ {الأنبياء/83} فَاسْتَجَبْنَا لَهُ فَكَشَفْنَا مَا بِهِ مِن ضُرٍّ وَآتَيْنَاهُ أَهْلَهُ وَمِثْلَهُم مَّعَهُمْ رَحْمَةً مِّنْ عِندِنَا وَذِكْرَى لِلْعَابِدِينَ {الأنبياء/84}

وَذَا النُّونِ إِذ ذَّهَبَ مُغَاضِبًا فَظَنَّ أَن لَّن نَّقْدِرَ عَلَيْهِ فَنَادَى فِي الظُّلُمَاتِ أَن لَّا إِلَهَ إِلَّا أَنتَ سُبْحَانَكَ إِنِّي كُنتُ مِنَ الظَّالِمِينَ {الأنبياء/87} فَاسْتَجَبْنَا لَهُ وَنَجَّيْنَاهُ مِنَ الْغَمِّ وَكَذَلِكَ نُنجِي الْمُؤْمِنِينَ {الأنبياء/88}

---

93. **[21:83]** And [mention] Job, when he called to his Lord, "Indeed, adversity has touched me, and you are the Most Merciful of the merciful." **[21:84]** So We responded to him and removed what afflicted him of adversity. And We gave him [back] his family and the like thereof with them as mercy from Us and a reminder for the worshippers [of Allah]. **[21:85]** And [mention] Ishmael and Idrees and Dhul-Kifl; all were of the patient. **[21:86]** And We admitted them into Our mercy. Indeed, they were of the righteous. **[21:87]** And [mention] the man of the fish, when he went off in anger and thought that We would not decree [anything] upon him. And he called out within the darknesses, "There is no deity except You; exalted are You. Indeed, I have been of the wrongdoers." **[21:88]** So We responded to him and saved him from the distress. And thus do We save the believers. **[21:89]** And [mention] Zechariah, when he called to his Lord, "My Lord, do not leave me alone [with no heir], while you are the best of inheritors." **[21:90]** So We responded to him, and We gave to him John, and amended for him his wife. Indeed, they used to hasten to good deeds and supplicate Us in hope and fear, and they were to Us humbly submissive.

وَزَكَرِيَّا إِذْ نَادَى رَبَّهُ رَبِّ لَا تَذَرْنِي فَرْدًا وَأَنتَ خَيْرُ الْوَارِثِينَ {89/الأنبياء} فَاسْتَجَبْنَا لَهُ وَوَهَبْنَا لَهُ يَحْيَى وَأَصْلَحْنَا لَهُ زَوْجَهُ إِنَّهُمْ كَانُوا يُسَارِعُونَ فِي الْخَيْرَاتِ وَيَدْعُونَنَا رَغَبًا وَرَهَبًا وَكَانُوا لَنَا خَاشِعِينَ
{90/الأنبياء}

أَللَّهُمَّ صَلِّ عَلَى سَيِّدِنَا وَ حَبِيْبَنَا مُحَمَّد ﷺ

Allahumma Salli ala Sayyidina wa Habibìna Muhammad ﷺ.

[107]⁹⁴

Challenges & Our Position

وَمَا أَرْسَلْنَاكَ إِلَّا رَحْمَةً لِّلْعَالَمِينَ
{107/الأنبياء}

One should remember that controlling one's tongue mostly start with controlling one's thoughts.

Assumptions, and projection of thoughts about others put the person in situations that a person may say something that can cause destructions in families, friendships and society.

We need to establish a methodology in ourselves for our thoughts. One of the best of this methodologies is to move beyond from the bad assumptions about people. If we are going to assume, then assuming well-being for others but not assumptions evil engagements for them. The highest stage of this methodology is that while recognizing others mistakes and faults but yet, still treating them with kindness, care and gentleness in order to help them remove these diseases.

Rasulullah ﷺ was always at the highest level of all the noble traits.

The ayah indicates this highest stagest of Rasulullah ﷺ as وَمَا أَرْسَلْنَاكَ إِلَّا رَحْمَةً لِّلْعَالَمِينَ {107/الأنبياء}

The word Rahmah in its absolute form is for Allah ﷻ.

Allah ﷻ knows, sees, and hears all our faults and spiritual sicknesses, yet Allah ﷻ still treats us with gentleness, care, kindness, and forgiveness.

To emphasize all this point, one can remember the opening of each Sûrah of the Qurãn with bismillãhiRahmãniRahìm with added emphasis of the Name of Allah ﷻ as al-Rahìm. To emphasize further

---

94. And We have not sent you, [O Muhammad], except as a mercy to the worlds.

this point, the short opening chapter of Sûrah Fātiha has the repetition of these Attributes of Allah ﷾.

One should know that one of the difficulties in life is if you know that a person is constantly faulty with different spiritual sicknesses of attitudes of belligerence, rudeness, not acceptance but always rejection with heedlessness, then this is extremely but extremely difficult still treating this person with gentleness, care, kindness, forgiveness and with a smile on the face.

The most clear form of this attitude of the person with Allah ﷾ is called kufr.

On one side Allah ﷾ knows everything of the person as al-Bātin and al-Zāhir, Allah ﷾ sees and witnesses everything of the person in private and in public as al-Khabir, al-Bāsir, al-Sami'u, yet the person acts in the extreme rudeness and belligerence of rejection his or her reality of existence by not recognizing Allah ﷾ truly and accordingly establishing not establishing a true and genuine connection with Allah ﷾.

May Allah ﷾ protect us.

When we consider the projection of this Attribute of Allah ﷾ as Rahman on humans, Rasulullah ﷺ has the highest form of display of this attribute of rahman as mentioned[95] {107/الأنبياء} وَمَا أَرْسَلْنَاكَ إِلَّا رَحْمَةً لِّلْعَالَمِينَ

Why and how?

When we review the life of Rasulullah ﷺ, Rasulullah ﷺ embodied this attribute as a human and as the messenger of Allah ﷾ in treatment of everyone and everything including animated and inanimate beings with gentleness, care, kindness, and forgiveness.

One can remember the pillar of the tree/wood post of the mosque of masjid nabawwi ﷺ. Rasulullah ﷺ tried to soothe and calm this pillar wood/tree post with his blessed hand ﷺ when its loud crying was heard in the mosque and witnessed by many [10].

This is an example of this utmost rahmah of Rasulullah ﷺ displayed about, as what we call, inanimate beings.

The mule coming to the Prophet ﷺ complaining and crying about its abuse by its owner is another example among animals. He ﷺ called the owner and warned the owner and the mule was relieved from this heavy duty [20].

---

95. And We have not sent you, [O Muhammad], except as a mercy to the worlds.

If above are examples from the beings of animated and inanimate beings about the display of rahmah of Rasulullah ﷺ, then one can ask how about the humans? There are thousands of examples in the life of Rasulullah ﷺ about his treatment of women, children, elderly, and everyone with rahmah.

Even in the cases of actions or attitudes deemed to be very inappropriate by all most all humans regardless of Muslims or non-Muslims, this unique position of the epitome of being Rahmatan lil A'lamin was always displayed and embodied by Rasululullah ﷺ.

To prove this point, let's take the example of the person urinating in the middle of the mosque [13] [10].

In the past and with all this inappropriate and immodest normalized popular actions of today, this action of urinating in the temple is still considered very inappropriate, rude, and extreme problematic.

Yet, when this incident happened in the blessed mosque of masjid nabawwi ﷺ, as the sahabah was about to rush to stop this person, Rasulullah ﷺ stopped them and said "let the man stop finish urinating and fulfill his need."

After, he finished his need, the prophet ﷺ poured a bucket of water on this human remnant to wash it away. Then, he ﷺ gently told him that the place that they are in, is a place of worship and they pray there. If a person needs to relieve oneself, there is another place for it [10]. After this incident, the man who did this action says that "at that time, the Prophet was the most beloved for me when I heard this from him with such gentleness while others were about to attack me" [10].

Now at our level, if take the challenge of treating people with gentleness, care and kindness especially when we know and recognize their mistakes and issues, do we really do it or not?

This happens a lot between children and parent relations.

This happens a lot among family members where one can display belligerent attitude toward another.

The can happen among brothers or sisters that one can be really showing some alternative motives of hurting the other.

This can happen in professional settings that a person may want to constantly dump the work on another person but avoiding his or her responsibility.

So, what do we do?

The best answer is to ask ourselves, by analyzing the sunnah and life of Rasulullah ﷺ in a similar situation, if Rasulullah ﷺ was at that position what would he ﷺ do?

Most of us know the answer. Yet, do we do it?

SubhanAllah!

May Allah ﷻ give us the character and ways of Rasulullah ﷺ in all our life engagements, Amìn.

اللهُمَّ صَلِّ على رَحْمَة للعَالَمِيْن المُصْطَفى ﷺ الف الف مَرّة، آمِيْن

Allahumma Salli ala Rahmatan lil A'lamin al-Mustafa ﷺ Alfu -Alfu Marra, Amìn

Sûrah 22 al-Hajj

[31-32]

Shirk, Worries & Anxiety

حُنَفَاء للَّهِ غَيْرَ مُشْرِكِينَ بِهِ وَمَن يُشْرِكْ باللَّهِ فَكَأَنَّمَا خَرَّ مِنَ السَّمَاء فَتَخْطَفُهُ الطَّيْرُ أَوْ تَهْوِي بِهِ الرِّيحُ فِي مَكَانٍ سَحِيقٍ 96}الحج/31{

One should remember that anything that causes the person uneasiness, stress, or worry can be a possibility of a shirk for the person in one's relationship with Allah ﷻ.

Imān requires taslìm, submission. Taslìm-submission requires tawakkul-reliance on Allah ﷻ.

A person being worried about a possible outcome of an incident can make things around that incident as a possible source of shirk. This is contrary to imān and tawhid.

Everything and every attachment other than Allah ﷻ is a source of pain, worry and grief for the person.

When we analyze this ayah, according to Sheikh Shārāwi [21], the sky implies Islām. Falling down is any type of shirk with a gravitational force of the nafs or nafs ammara-evil rendering nafs. The person falls down from the high noble position of Islām that requires imān, tawakkul and ihsān as mentioned خَرَّ مِنَ السَّمَاء.

---

96. Inclining [only] to Allah, not associating [anything] with Him. And he who associates with Allah - it is as though he had fallen from the sky and was snatched by the birds or the wind carried him down into a remote place.

The catching of the birds is the shāwat portion of the nafs as mentioned فَتَخْطَفُهُ الطَّيْرُ. Here, the word فَتَخْطَفُهُ can indicate an immediate grasp like shāwāt of lust, anger, food and others. The wind can indicate the wind and all the evil whisperings of Shaytān taking the person to different unknown darkness as mentioned تَهْوِي بِهِ الرِّيحُ فِي مَكَانٍ سَحِيقٍ

One should remember that any worry is a possible source of shirk for the person. One should really turn to Allah ﷻ with dua, ikhlās for constantly asking and having the true tawhid of imān in the heart and mind as mentioned حُنَفَاءَ لِلّٰهِ غَيْرَ مُشْرِكِينَ بِهِ.

Whoever claims to have imān but yet makes shirk as mentioned وَمَن يُشْرِكْ بِاللّٰهِ, then the above psychological renderings of pain, anguish, uneasiness, stress, worry, agitation, losing the sleep, defocus and all other chaotic states of the mind and heart can overpower the person. This is due to shirk of expecting and turning to the things even slightly other than only Allah ﷻ.

Yet, this is sometimes very difficult to detect. Riyā-showing off is a shirk. Yet, it is difficult to detect this shirk similar to a dark ant in a dark room as mentioned by Rasulullah 7] ﷺ].

So, what do we do?

We should be constantly monitoring hearts similar to the EKG machines. Yet, this monitoring of the heart should be at each second not when the person is need in a hospital.

The spiritual diseases of shirk affecting directly the heart can kill the person at any time. Then, we may see people on earth suffering the punishment of hell with anxiety, fear, stress, uneasiness before they die. Yet, the more sorrow ending may be after death. May Allah ﷻ protect us.

It is interesting to note that "sky is falling" is an idiom in English to emphasize highest level of stress, SubhanAllah.

The source of this idiom can be biblical but yet as we think about this ayah a person falling from the sky and this idiom as "sky is falling" in its opposite reference point to indicate a very stressed person who is in the psychological states of stress, terror and anguish. It is very interesting to realize very amazing depictions of the Qurān to display vividly human's psychological states.

Today, when we analyze today's engagement of skydiving with the perspective of this ayah. Skydiving is defined as "the sport of jumping from an aircraft and performing acrobatic maneuvers in the air during free fall before landing by parachute" [1].

Another term that comes a lot with skydiving is phobia defined as "an extreme or irrational fear of or aversion to something," [1].

It shows from some of the research published by Pennsylvania state university titled as "The Psychology of Being Human" that novice skydivers report that the first day of jumping in air was the "the most terrifying experiences of their lives" [21]. The ones who are experienced in skydiving have increased anxiety and fear from the morning of that day and their fear did not peak until they were airborne [21].

This shows that even experienced skydivers fear much.

In the depictions of the Qurān, when one visualizes this possible jumping, the fear factor with anxiety, terror, anguish are realities with the engagements of the person with shirk.

Shirk is any expectation of the person other than Allah ﷻ and any fear associated with it as an end product . This state and engagement can cause worse than the fears of skydiving.

May Allah ﷻ protect us Amīn and give us imān, Islām, tawakkul and taslīm, Amīn.

اللهُمَّ صَلِّ على سيدنا محمد ﷺ و على آل سيدنا محمد كما صليت على سيدنا إبراهيم وعلى آل إبراهيم إنك حميد مجيد

Allahumma Salli ala Sayyidina Muhammad ﷺ wa a'la a'li Sayyidina Muhammad kama sallayta a'lā ibrāhīm wa a'la alī ibrāhīm innaka Hāmidun Mājīd.

[32]⁹⁷

Shirk & Respecting the Shi'ār of Allah ﷻ

ذَلِكَ وَمَن يُعَظِّمْ شَعَائِرَ اللَّهِ فَإِنَّهَا مِن تَقْوَى الْقُلُوبِ
{الحج/32}

When we consider this ayah with the previous ayah, one can realize there is a fine line with true tawhid and respecting and engaging with attitudes, rituals, worship and 'ibadah due to its relation with Allah ﷻ.

The previous ayah underlines being a hanif only turning to Allah ﷻ without making any shirk to Allah ﷻ as mentioned حُنَفَاء لِلَّهِ غَيْرَ مُشْرِكِينَ بِهِ.

---

97. That [is so]. And whoever honors the symbols of Allah - indeed, it is from the piety of hearts.

Yet, this ayah indicates after establishing and constantly remembering and embodying بِهِ, حُنَفَاء لِلَّهِ غَيْرَ مُشْرِكِينَ, then one should embody the orders, rituals and all engagements that are related with Allah ﷻ as mentioned يُعَظِّمْ شَعَائِرَ اللَّهِ

In other words, the real sign or application of the teaching of حُنَفَاء لِلَّهِ is يُعَظِّمْ شَعَائِرَ اللَّهِ غَيْرَ مُشْرِكِينَ بِهِ.

Here is the real problem that we encounter in implementation of حُنَفَاء لِلَّهِ غَيْرَ مُشْرِكِينَ بِهِ. We find people who may say "I just worship Allah ﷻ. I don't care about the prophets, books or other teachings." Most of the problematic cases may not be as obvious as this but today, people may see groups that may say "we don't follow the sunnah, or teachings of the Prophet ﷺ. We only follow the Qurān." This problematic approach can dismiss the order in[98] ذَلِكَ وَمَن يُعَظِّمْ شَعَائِرَ اللَّه فَإِنَّهَا مِن تَقْوَى الْقُلُوبِ {الحج/32}

One should remember that the biggest shiār of Allah ﷻ is the Qurān, Rasulullah ﷺ, and teachings of Rasulullah ﷺ.

There is an entire discussion in the scholarship if La ilaha illa Allah is sufficient with out Muhammadun Rasulullah. The consensus is that if the person by choice and purpose excludes Muhammadun Rasulullah, then the pleasure of Allah ﷻ in this life and afterlife is really questionable.

When the person does not adapt the primary shiār such as Rasulullah ﷺ and sunnah of Rasulullah ﷺ, and the people and the teachings around them, then there can be the real issue of not implementing وَمَن يُعَظِّمْ شَعَائِرَ اللَّهِ.

Then, one cannot talk about taqwa. There is no taqwa.

The fruit of this application of يُعَظِّمْ شَعَائِرَ اللَّهِ is تَقْوَى الْقُلُوبِ.

One should remember that Shaytān did not implement the teaching of وَمَن يُعَظِّمْ شَعَائِرَ اللَّهِ. Allah ﷻ ordered Shaytān to have respect to Adam as. Shaytān disrespected Allah ﷻ by not following the order of respecting Adam as by going against the teaching of وَمَن يُعَظِّمْ شَعَائِرَ اللَّهِ.

In that sense, Shaytān did not have taqwa in his heart.

May Allah ﷻ protect in our engagements of not following وَمَن يُعَظِّمْ شَعَائِرَ اللَّهِ, Amìn

May Allah ﷻ give us taqwa, Amìn

أَللَّهُمَّ صَلِّ عَلَى سَيِّدِنَا وَ حَبِيْبَنَا مُحَمّد ﷺ

---

98. That [is so]. And whoever honors the symbols of Allah - indeed, it is from the piety of hearts.

Allahumma Salli A'la Sayyidina wa Habibina Muhammad wa a'la alihi wa Sahbihi Ajmain.

[39]⁹⁹

Prophets & Peace

أُذِنَ لِلَّذِينَ يُقَاتَلُونَ بِأَنَّهُمْ ظُلِمُوا وَإِنَّ اللَّهَ عَلَى نَصْرِهِمْ لَقَدِيرٌ
{الحج/39}

One should remember fighting is not essence in Islām. When we analyze the ayah the word أُذِنَ can indicate the norm form peace. The word أُذِنَ can indicate a permission as an exception. As an exception, defending oneself against oppression is permitted in Islām.

One can remember that there were cases in the past who were friends of Allah ﷻ, they preferred not to defend themselves. In the external looking of evil seeming incidents, they were killed and oppressed. Yet, in the unseen world of the real realities, they were in the highest maqām of being in peace and happiness. This is mentioned as¹⁰⁰ قِيلَ ادْخُلِ الْجَنَّةَ قَالَ يَا لَيْتَ قَوْمِي يَعْلَمُونَ {يس/26}

According to tafāsir, one of the ahlullah referred as Najjār (رحمه الله) was martyred due to his reminders to his people about the truthful teachings of the prophets. Then, he was immediately accepted Jannah as soon as he was killed as mentioned قِيلَ ادْخُلِ الْجَنَّةَ قَالَ يَا لَيْتَ قَوْمِي يَعْلَمُونَ {يس/26}.

One can analyze the two verses as¹⁰¹ إِنِّي آمَنتُ بِرَبِّكُمْ فَاسْمَعُونِ {يس/25} قِيلَ ادْخُلِ الْجَنَّةَ قَالَ يَا لَيْتَ قَوْمِي يَعْلَمُونَ {يس/26}

There is no conjugation or explanation between ayahs 25 and 26 as one can also call this that there is a mahzūf in Qurānic sciences. Yet, on another perspective, there seemed to be a rush to kill this ahlullah (رحمه الله) when he (رحمه الله) gave them some nasihah-reminder about the trustful and truthful disposition of these messengers of Allah ﷻ. Yet, the rush of these oppressors to kill this ahlullah (رحمه الله) transformed a rush of his immediate entrance to Jannah as one can realize that there is

---

99. Permission [to fight] has been given to those who are being fought, because they were wronged. And indeed, Allah is competent to give them victory.
100. It was said, "Enter Paradise." He said, "I wish my people could know
101. [36:25] Indeed, I have believed in your Lord, so listen to me." [36:26] It was said, "Enter Paradise." He said, "I wish my people could know

no conjunction or further explanation between two ayahs (26 & 25). The immediate result is presented, Allahu A'lam.

May Allah ﷻ make us from the ahlullah, Amìn

May Allah ﷻ embody the path of the Prophets and the people of Allah ﷻ (ahlullah), Amìn.

May Allah ﷻ make us enter Jannah without any hasāb immediately as soon as we die in gentle way with the Divine Karam, Lutf, and Grace, Amìn.

اَللّٰهُمَّ صَلِّ عَلَى سَيِّدِنَا وَ حَبِيبِنَا مُحَمَّد ﷺ

Allahumma Salli a'lā Sayyidina wa Habìbinā Muhammad ﷺ.

Juz 19

Sûrah 25 al-Furqān

[77]

Dua and the Real Reality of Our Existence & Purpose

قُلْ مَا يَعْبَأُ بِكُمْ رَبِّي لَوْلَا دُعَاؤُكُمْ فَقَدْ كَذَّبْتُمْ فَسَوْفَ يَكُونُ لِزَامًا
{الفرقان/77}

One should know the person needs Allah ﷻ at all times. Making dua to Allah ﷻ is the acceptance and activation of the this need of the person.

The need of dua to Allah ﷻ constantly in five times prayers, nawāfil, outside the prayers, walking, sitting, thinking and sleeping is a dare need and reality.

The person fully should understand that he or she cannot do anything and achieve a real result without the opening and enablement from Allah ﷻ.

The eyes of the person should constantly cry, and the heart of the person should constantly be thirsty and hungry to turn to Allah ﷻ. The constant turning of the person to Allah ﷻ is called dua.

We have a lot of problems constantly, each second, each minute, and each day. Yet, we don't set aside a time to focus on these problems with dua to Allah ﷻ.

One should remember that dua is the pillar of solving all problems and the rest of reasons and causalities are built on this pillar.

If the pillar is not there, regardless of the quality and expensive prices of the windows or decoration, the building will collapse.

Following the causalities and reasons without true turning to Allah ﷻ with dua will be all abtar, fruitless.

In our terminology having a fruit includes continuation of the blessings in this life and afterlife as mentioned كُلَّمَا رُزِقُواْ مِنْهَا مِن ثَمَرَةٍ رِّزْقاً in وَبَشِّرِ الَّذِين آمَنُواْ وَعَمِلُواْ الصَّالِحَاتِ أَنَّ لَهُمْ قَالُواْ هَذَا الَّذِي رُزِقْنَا مِن قَبْلُ وَأُتُواْ بِهِ مُتَشَابِهاً جَنَّاتٍ تَجْرِي مِن تَحْتِهَا الأَنْهَارُ كُلَّمَا رُزِقُواْ مِنْهَا مِن ثَمَرَةٍ رِّزْقاً قَالُواْ هَذَا الَّذِي رُزِقْنَا مِن قَبْلُ وَأُتُواْ بِهِ مُتَشَابِهاً وَلَهُمْ فِيهَا أَزْوَاجٌ مُطَهَّرَةٌ وَهُمْ فِيهَا خَالِدُونَ {البقرة/25} [102]

If there is no dua to Allah ﷻ, there is no real fruit.

If there is no dua, there is no real solving and achievement of the real results.

One can ask: is dua humiliating or necessary at all times?

One should remember that dua is the essence of our existence.

Being A'bd of Allah ﷻ requires the dare need for Allah ﷻ.

Being A'bd of Allah ﷻ requires realization of one's need as a limited human being and asking all the needs from Allah ﷻ.

Therefore, if the person does not have any dua, actually his or her existence in life is useless or purposeless and not according to his or her purpose.

If the person does not turn to Allah ﷻ with dua, he or she turns other things as deity or deities with kufr instead of Allah ﷻ.

These deities can be his or her own self called ego or nafs. Sometimes, there can be added deities such as wealth, position, or other humans. All these deities are fake and not real.

The turning of the person to his or her own ego as a deity is due to the filthy spiritual sickness of arrogance.

Arrogance blocks the reality of the dua of the person for Allah ﷻ.

Yet, this blocking is temporary and shattered harshly with realities due to the human's real disposition of weakness.

There are a lot of people claiming deities due to their arrogance but their claims are all destroyed with loss of health, wealth or the loved ones as their dependent deities.

May Allah ﷻ protect us, Amìn.

---

102. And give good tidings to those who believe and do righteous deeds that they will have gardens [in Paradise] beneath which rivers flow. Whenever they are provided with a provision of fruit therefrom, they will say, "This is what we were provided with before." And it is given to them in likeness. And they will have therein purified spouses, and they will abide therein eternally.

Therefore, evil-seeming incidents serve a purpose in each individual's life.

Yet, we ask Allah ﷻ to treat us with Lutf, Kindness and Care and help us to remove the implicit or explicit shirk from our hearts with self-realization but without being exposed to these devastating trials or tests.

Amìn.

Here is an example of Karûn in the Qurãn with his statement:[103]

قَالَ إِنَّمَا أُوتِيتُهُ عَلَى عِلْمٍ عِندِي أَوَلَمْ يَعْلَمْ أَنَّ اللَّهَ قَدْ أَهْلَكَ مِن قَبْلِهِ مِنَ الْقُرُونِ مَنْ هُوَ أَشَدُّ مِنْهُ قُوَّةً وَأَكْثَرُ جَمْعًا وَلَا يُسْأَلُ عَن ذُنُوبِهِمُ الْمُجْرِمُونَ {القصص/78}

Here is the disastrous destruction of his deities[104]

فَخَسَفْنَا بِهِ وَبِدَارِهِ الْأَرْضَ فَمَا كَانَ لَهُ مِن فِئَةٍ يَنصُرُونَهُ مِن دُونِ اللَّهِ وَمَا كَانَ مِنَ الْمُنتَصِرِينَ {القصص/81}

Here is the example of Firawn in the Qurãn:[105]

وَقَالَ فِرْعَوْنُ يَا أَيُّهَا الْمَلَأُ مَا عَلِمْتُ لَكُم مِّنْ إِلَهٍ غَيْرِي فَأَوْقِدْ لِي يَا هَامَانُ عَلَى الطِّينِ فَاجْعَل لِّي صَرْحًا لَّعَلِّي أَطَّلِعُ إِلَى إِلَهِ مُوسَى وَإِنِّي لَأَظُنُّهُ مِنَ الْكَاذِبِينَ {القصص/38}

Here is the doomed annihilation of this deity:[106]

فَأَخَذْنَاهُ وَجُنُودَهُ فَنَبَذْنَاهُمْ فِي الْيَمِّ فَانظُرْ كَيْفَ كَانَ عَاقِبَةُ الظَّالِمِينَ {القصص/40}

The matter is serious.
The journey is short.
Our time is ending.

---

103. He said, "I was only given it because of knowledge I have." Did he not know that Allah had destroyed before him of generations those who were greater than him in power and greater in accumulation [of wealth]? But the criminals, about their sins, will not be asked.
104. And We caused the earth to swallow him and his home. And there was for him no company to aid him other than Allah, nor was he of those who [could] defend themselves.
105. And Pharaoh said, "O eminent ones, I have not known you to have a god other than me. Then ignite for me, O Haman, [a fire] upon the clay and make for me a tower that I may look at the God of Moses. And indeed, I do think he is among the liars."
106. So We took him and his soldiers and threw them into the sea. So see how was the end of the wrongdoers.

May Allah ﷻ remove from our hearts with lutf the traces of arrogance before we die, Amìn

May Allah ﷻ make us constantly and sincerely turn with dua to Allah ﷻ as a habit without the need of reminders of trials, and tests, Amìn.

May Allah ﷻ make us follow the path of al-Habìb ﷺ , the Most Loved By Allah ﷻ and make us love the ones who Allah ﷻ loves and Rasulullah ﷺ loves, Amìn

May Allah ﷻ protect us claiming explicit or implicit deities on the path of Allah ﷻ and doing the work of the dìn but in loss the person is in reality, Amìn.

اللهُمَّ صَلِّ عَلَى سَيِّدِنَا وَ حَبِيْبَنَا وَ إِمَامَنَا وَمَوْلَانَا مُحَمّد ﷺ

Allahumma Salli ala Sayyidina wa Habìbina wa Imāmana wa Mawlana Muhammad ﷺ

Juz 20

Sûrah 28 al-Qasas

[4]¹⁰⁷

Cruelty Realities and Power of Imãn

إِنَّ فِرْعَوْنَ عَلَا فِي الْأَرْضِ وَجَعَلَ أَهْلَهَا شِيَعًا يَسْتَضْعِفُ طَائِفَةً مِّنْهُمْ يُذَبِّحُ أَبْنَاءهُمْ وَيَسْتَحْيِي نِسَاءهُمْ إِنَّهُ كَانَ مِنَ الْمُفْسِدِينَ {القصص/4}

فَلَمَّا جَاءهُم بِالْحَقِّ مِنْ عِندِنَا قَالُوا اقْتُلُوا أَبْنَاء الَّذِينَ آمَنُوا مَعَهُ وَاسْتَحْيُوا نِسَاءهُمْ وَمَا كَيْدُ الْكَافِرِينَ إِلَّا فِي ضَلَالٍ ¹⁰⁸{غافر/25}

One should remember that Allah is al-Adl, All-Just. When we look at incidents externally from its cover, we seem to deduce injustice in evil-seeming incidents. Then, some people question, astagfirullah, the Attribute of Allah ﷻ as al-Adl. Astagfirullah. Then, some people alienate and isolate themselves from religious teachings, religion and group or

---

107. Indeed, Pharaoh exalted himself in the land and made its people into factions, oppressing a sector among them, slaughtering their [newborn] sons and keeping their females alive. Indeed, he was of the corrupters.
108. And when he brought them the truth from Us, they said, "Kill the sons of those who have believed with him and keep their women alive." But the plan of the disbelievers is not except in error.

religious institutional affiliations. This happened a lot among Christians and Jews and now, happening among Muslims.

When we analyze the above ayahs, there is an apparent evil seeming incident of killing children and killing people. Yet, everyone's accountability is with Allah ﷻ and everyone's return is with Allah ﷻ. We don't know in this horrifying incidents Allah ﷻ could make these places a place of Jannah like Allah ﷻ did it for Ibrahim as mentioned as[109] يَا قُلْنَا

نَارُ كُونِي بَرْدًا وَسَلَامًا عَلَى إِبْرَاهِيمَ {الأنبياء/69}.

Yet, we are humans. We judge, feel sorrow and become sad with externalities. Allah ﷻ knows the reality of internalities as Al-Bāṭin and Al-Ẓāhir.

When we hear

▶ that humans and Muslims are being tortured and placed in the prisons without any reason but due to their beliefs and affiliations,

▶ that women are placed in the prisons without any reason but only being a Muslim in a group,

▶ that new born children are placed in the prison with their mothers, then

we can't help but we cry and cry, and ask ourselves what we could do against the tyranny of people with oppression.

This happened in the past as mentioned in the above ayahs and as also mentioned in[110] وَالسَّمَاءِ ذَاتِ الْبُرُوجِ {البروج/1} وَالْيَوْمِ الْمَوْعُودِ {البروج/2} وَشَاهِدٍ وَمَشْهُودٍ {البروج/3} قُتِلَ أَصْحَابُ الْأُخْدُودِ {البروج/4} النَّارِ ذَاتِ الْوَقُودِ {البروج/5} إِذْ هُمْ عَلَيْهَا قُعُودٌ {البروج/6} وَهُمْ عَلَى مَا يَفْعَلُونَ بِالْمُؤْمِنِينَ شُهُودٌ {البروج/7} وَمَا نَقَمُوا مِنْهُمْ إِلَّا أَن يُؤْمِنُوا بِاللَّهِ الْعَزِيزِ الْحَمِيدِ {البروج/8} الَّذِي لَهُ مُلْكُ السَّمَاوَاتِ وَالْأَرْضِ وَاللَّهُ عَلَى كُلِّ شَيْءٍ شَهِيدٌ {البروج/9} إِنَّ الَّذِينَ فَتَنُوا الْمُؤْمِنِينَ وَالْمُؤْمِنَاتِ ثُمَّ لَمْ يَتُوبُوا فَلَهُمْ عَذَابُ جَهَنَّمَ وَلَهُمْ عَذَابُ الْحَرِيقِ {البروج/10}

Unfortunately, it is happening today.

---

109. Allah said, "O fire, be coolness and safety upon Abraham."

110. **1.** By the sky containing great stars **2.** And [by] the promised Day **3.** And [by] the witness and what is witnessed,**4.** Destroyed [i.e., cursed] were the companions of the trench.**5.** [Containing] the fire full of fuel,**6.** When they were sitting near it**7.** And they, to what they were doing against the believers, were witnesses.**8.** And they resented them not except because they believed in Allah, the Exalted in Might, the Praiseworthy,**9.** To whom belongs the dominion of the heavens and the earth. And Allah, over all things, is Witness.**10.** Indeed, those who have tortured the believing men and believing women and then have not repented will have the punishment of Hell, and they will have the punishment of the Burning Fire.

The first place for seeking solution at all times and at this time is turning to Allah ﷻ with dua.

Then, one can think of means of helping people with a good word, hope, and any means to relieve their pain. In reality, they may not be in pain but in the breezes of Jannah like Ibrahim as. Yet, we as humans judge with externalities. Allah ﷻ knows the internalities.

One should remember that one should not lose hope at all times even he or she is alone by him or herself and even if all the world is against this person. This is the power of imān when the person leans oneself to Allah ﷻ Who is All Powerful, Al-Qādir. This is tawakkul-reliance to Allah ﷻ.

اللهُمَّ إغْفِرِالمؤمِنِيْنَ والمؤمنات، آمِيْن

اللهُمَّ أرحَم أمة مُحمد ﷺ بِحُرْمَةِ رسُوْل الله ﷺ، آمِيْن

اللهُمَّ صَلِّ عَلَى سَيِّدِنَا وَ حَبِيْبَنَا مُحَمّد ﷺ الف الف مرة في هذه الساعة وكل آن، آمِين

Allahumma Agfirlil Mu'minina wal Mu'minat, Amìn,

Allahumma Arham Ummata Muhammad ﷺ bi Hurmati Rasulullah ﷺ, Amìn

Allahumma Salli Ala Sayyidina wa Habibina Muhammad ﷺ Alfu Alfu Marrah fi hazihi sa'ah wa kullil āʾn, Amìn.

[15-19][111]

Fear with Unexpected Incidents & the Claims of Our Free Will as Source of the Problems

وَدَخَلَ الْمَدِينَةَ عَلَى حِينِ غَفْلَةٍ مِّنْ أَهْلِهَا فَوَجَدَ فِيهَا رَجُلَيْنِ يَقْتَتِلَانِ هَذَا مِن شِيعَتِهِ وَهَذَا مِنْ عَدُوِّهِ فَاسْتَغَاثَهُ الَّذِي مِن شِيعَتِهِ عَلَى الَّذِي مِنْ عَدُوِّهِ فَوَكَزَهُ مُوسَى فَقَضَى عَلَيْهِ قَالَ هَذَا مِنْ عَمَلِ الشَّيْطَانِ إِنَّهُ عَدُوٌّ مُّضِلٌّ مُّبِينٌ {القصص/15} قَالَ رَبِّ إِنِّي ظَلَمْتُ نَفْسِي فَاغْفِرْ لِي فَغَفَرَ لَهُ إِنَّهُ هُوَ الْغَفُورُ الرَّحِيمُ {القصص/16} قَالَ رَبِّ بِمَا أَنْعَمْتَ

---

111. **15.** And he entered the city at a time of inattention by its people and found therein two men fighting: one from his faction and one from among his enemy. And the one from his faction called for help to him against the one from his enemy, so Moses struck him and [unintentionally] killed him. [Moses] said, "This is from the work of Satan. Indeed, he is a manifest, misleading enemy." **16.** He said, "My Lord, indeed I have wronged myself, so forgive me," and He forgave him. Indeed, He is the Forgiving, the Merciful. **17.** He said, "My Lord, for the favor You bestowed upon me, I will never be an assistant to the criminals." **18.** And he became inside the city fearful and anticipating [exposure],when suddenly the one who sought his help the previous day cried out to him [once again]. Moses said to him, "Indeed, you are an evident, [persistent] deviator."

عَلَيَّ فَلَنْ أَكُونَ ظَهِيرًا لِّلْمُجْرِمِينَ {القصص/17} فَأَصْبَحَ فِي الْمَدِينَةِ خَائِفًا يَتَرَقَّبُ فَإِذَا الَّذِي اسْتَنصَرَهُ بِالْأَمْسِ يَسْتَصْرِخُهُ قَالَ لَهُ مُوسَى إِنَّكَ لَغَوِيٌّ مُّبِينٌ {القصص/18} فَلَمَّا أَنْ أَرَادَ أَن يَبْطِشَ بِالَّذِي هُوَ عَدُوٌّ لَّهُمَا قَالَ يَا مُوسَى أَتُرِيدُ أَن تَقْتُلَنِي كَمَا قَتَلْتَ نَفْسًا بِالْأَمْسِ إِن تُرِيدُ إِلَّا أَن تَكُونَ جَبَّارًا فِي الْأَرْضِ وَمَا تُرِيدُ أَن تَكُونَ مِنَ الْمُصْلِحِينَ {{القصص/19}

One should remember to constantly to turn Allah ﷻ for the unexpected trials and tests that can instill different states of spiritual disturbance in one's heart and mind.

One of the sources of this spiritual disturbance is from khawf-fear.

One can review the incident of Musa (عليه السلام) mentioned in the sets of ayahs above. Musa (عليه السلام) wants to help someone, and a trial and a test occurs with the death of a person in this engagement. Then, a khawf displays in Musa (عليه السلام) mentioned فَأَصْبَحَ فِي الْمَدِينَةِ خَائِفًا.

Sometimes, in life we find ourselves in very petty situations that can result in big problems, disturbance and fear.

Yet, one should remember that we are all humans. These situations are all means for us to turn to Allah ﷻ as mentioned قَالَ رَبِّ إِنِّي ظَلَمْتُ نَفْسِي فَاغْفِرْ لِي فَغَفَرَ لَهُ إِنَّهُ هُوَ الْغَفُورُ الرَّحِيمُ {القصص/16} قَالَ رَبِّ بِمَا أَنْعَمْتَ عَلَيَّ فَلَنْ أَكُونَ ظَهِيرًا لِّلْمُجْرِمِينَ {القصص/17}.

Yes, we look at ourselves what we can do and what we can control in our limited problematic free will renderings and engagements.

One of the ahlullah of our time [18] makes the resemblance of this limited free will causing constantly problems similar a tiny flash light giving a very dim light and not working properly. The person relies on this flash light but yet, this flash light always causes problems instead of assistance.

This light really doesn't help the person to see but causes more problems. Yet, the person thinks that he or she sees with his or her flashlight and have pseudo confidence. This fake confidence sourced and backed up with arrogance of this person representing a very dim flashlight causes more and more problems in one's life.

Then, one day, this person gets sick of all the problems caused by this dim and tiny flashlight and says "I don't need this, it always caused problems in my life, I rather be blind and turn to Allah ﷻ instead of trusting this dim tiny flash light." Then, he smashes this tiny flashlight on the floor and as soon as he does that all the room, house, town, city, country, world, and universe gets a very powerful light as if he turned on a switch of a electric power.

Yes, this dim and tiny flash light is our nafs-ego deeming confidence and arrogance with a tiny and minuscule sizes of our free-will claiming power. This microscopic size of free will is not there to claim deity or power with arrogance but to recognize the miniscule size of its capacity in front of Rabbul A'lamìn Who is al-Qãdir, All-Powerful.

When the person recognizes this absolute reality of its minuscule limit in front of Greatness of Rabbul A'lamin ﷻ, then he actually gets power by leaning on the One Who is All Powerful, al-Bãki, Infinite, Allah ﷻ.

Yes, we should all break our misleading tiny flashlights of free will of ego and nafs by breaking its idols of claiming deity, superiority, judgment and arrogance.

In this regard, in classical understanding of iconism or idolatry, there is the ego and nafs that people are implicitly idolizing their own selves of ego, superiority, judgment and arrogance. They are not accepting who has the Real Uluhiyyah as instructed by the Scriptures such as the Qurãn, Tawrah, or Injil, and their primary and initial teachers of the prophets. Rather, they say explicitly and implicitly as "We don't need anyone to tell us Who has the Uluhiyyah or Who is Rahman" as mentioned[112] وَإِذَا قِيلَ لَهُمُ اسْجُدُوا لِلرَّحْمَنِ قَالُوا وَمَا الرَّحْمَنُ أَنَسْجُدُ لِمَا تَأْمُرُنَا وَزَادَهُمْ نُفُورًا {الفرقان/60}) (سجدة مستحبة)

SubhanAllah! This above ayah is an ayah of sajdah. The people of imãn who broke their deities immediately accept this reality and go to sajdah in the recication of above ayahs and other similar ayahs. Our salah includes sajdah to in order to constantly break our deities forming and trying to capture our nafs and ego.

Sajdah to Allah ﷻ is the symbol of breaking one's deity represented by the misleading flashlight of free will constantly pumping the air of arrogance. The air really does not have much mass but only volume. In other words, a balloon looks big with its size but it doesn't have much mass. The balloon itself thinks that it is big but a tiny prick is sufficient for its disappearance of its reality.

---

112. And when it is said to them, "Prostrate to the Most Merciful," they say, "And what is the Most Merciful? Should we prostrate to that which you order us?" And it increases them in aversion.

Therefore, Shaytān did not make sajdah for an order from Allah ﷻ. He was crushed under his minute flashlight of free-will instead of him crushing his own free will.

May Allah ﷻ protect us, Amìn.

For the person of imān, we still have the effects of this misleading flashlight of nafs and ego. Then, the case of khawf occurs as a natural outcome.

One should remember that Allah ﷻ is al-Bāki and al-Qādir. When a person is scared from something, and someone and if all the world comes against this person, a person of imān who truly and fully smashed and destroyed their flashlight of free will of nafs and ago leaning to Allah ﷻ does not panic, does not allow the breezes of fears being inhaled where everyone and everything is telling him or her to be fearful.

SubhanAllah!

The One Who is in Charge of everything, the One keeps this earth rotating and spinning in different orbits and axis with thousands of miles without us feeling these enormous motions, can do anything at any time.

For us, our lives our temporary and limited but gains value by our full reliance on Allah ﷻ with a high purpose goal seeded with imān.

During the constant waves of life, in each day with trials and tests, our emotions represent an ocean becoming wavy, calm, with wind or without wind. Yet, the only way is always to go to Allah ﷻ and realize that La Hawla wa la Quwwata illa Billah is the real power breaking our old tiny misleading flashlight and connecting to the source of the Electric Power of Light.

May Allah ﷻ make us realize and apply these realities before we damage ourselves with stress, fear, pessimism, anxiety and stress, Amìn

May Allah ﷻ empty our hearts and mind with all the deities that we implicitly and explicitly attach ourselves other than Allah ﷻ,

May Allah ﷻ give us the hilm, forbearance and gentleness of Rasulullah ﷺ as he ﷺ was sent as the Rahmah, Amìn

أَللهُمَّ صَلِّ عَلَى سَيِّدِنَا وَ حَبِيْبِنَا مُحَمّد ﷺ، المصطفى ﷺ

Allahumma Salli ala Sayyidina wa Habìibina Muhammad ﷺ, al-Mustafa ﷺ

[20-21][113]

Spiritual Diseases & Running to Allah ﷻ

وَجَاءَ رَجُلٌ مِّنْ أَقْصَى الْمَدِينَةِ يَسْعَى قَالَ يَا مُوسَى إِنَّ الْمَلَأَ يَأْتَمِرُونَ بِكَ لِيَقْتُلُوكَ فَاخْرُجْ إِنِّي لَكَ مِنَ النَّاصِحِينَ {القصص/20} فَخَرَجَ مِنْهَا خَائِفًا يَتَرَقَّبُ قَالَ رَبِّ نَجِّنِي مِنَ الْقَوْمِ الظَّالِمِينَ {القصص/21}

One should remember that we are weak and anything can happen at any time. This anything can be the death of the person, a sickness, a deserved or undeserved blame, attack of humans, Shayātin, or Jinn or anything.

In this regard, going back to Allah ﷻ every second with dua, remembrance of Allah ﷻ, Dhikrullah and other means of connecting with Allah ﷻ with the embodiment of La hawla wa la quwwata illa Billah is very critical.

When we take this fight personally on our weak shoulders, then actually we crack ourselves more with our weak stamina. But, when we turn ourselves fully and sincerely to Allah ﷻ, knowing that we are weak, then we receive an immediate relief and lightness on heart, mind and body.

All the forms of spiritual diseases such as jealousy, arrogance, vanity, conceit and all others are some representations of taking a burden on our weak selves of ego or nafs and making temporal or permanent identities with these diseases.

May Allah ﷻ protect us, Amìn.

Sometimes, a person on the path of helping others or giving service in order to please Allah ﷻ, the One, the person can be trapped with these diseases.

Then, the means become the ends for this person.

May Allah ﷻ protect us, Amìn

---

113. **[28:20]** And a man came from the farthest end of the city, running. He said, "O Moses, indeed the eminent ones are conferring over you [intending] to kill you, so leave [the city]; indeed, I am to you of the sincere advisors."
[28:21] So he left it, fearful and anticipating [apprehension]. He said, "My Lord, save me from the wrongdoing people."

Yes, it is a reality that there can be and there are people who can have bad and ill intentions to hurt the person.

Yet, this knowledge can increase the person's fear and vulnerability with unease, discomfort and agitation if he or she does not how to exit or response to these feelings accumulated with this knowledge or news.

When a person knows or feels that there is a potential harm from other things or beings, then the exit is to run to Allah ﷻ both from the physical and spiritual oppression of the people.

When Musa as was informed about the plot against him, he as both spiritually and physically run to Allah ﷻ as mentioned[114] وَجَاءَ رَجُلٌ مِّنْ أَقْصَى الْمَدِينَةِ يَسْعَى قَالَ يَا مُوسَى إِنَّ الْمَلَأَ يَأْتَمِرُونَ بِكَ لِيَقْتُلُوكَ فَاخْرُجْ إِنِّي لَكَ مِنَ النَّاصِحِينَ {القصص/20} فَخَرَجَ مِنْهَا خَائِفًا يَتَرَقَّبُ قَالَ رَبِّ نَجِّنِي مِنَ الْقَوْمِ الظَّالِمِينَ {القصص/21}

May Allah ﷻ make us to remember to run back to Allah ﷻ constantly and do not make us take us the burdens of life on our weak shoulders, Amìn

أَللَّهُمَّ صَلِّ على سَيِّدِنا مُحَمَّد وعلى آله سيدنا محمد كَمَا صَلَّيْتَ على سَيِّدِنا إبراهيم وعلى آل سيدنا إبراهيم إنك حميد مجيد

Allahumma Salli A'la Sayyidina Muhammad wa a'lā a'lì Sayyidina Muhammad kama Sallayta a'la Sayyidina Ibrahìm wa a'la a'lì Ibrahìm Innaka Hāmidun Majìd.

Juz 21

Sûrah 30 al-Rûm

[23][115]

Everyday's Motivational Milestones

وَمِنْ آيَاتِهِ مَنَامُكُم بِاللَّيْلِ وَالنَّهَارِ وَابْتِغَاؤُكُم مِّن فَضْلِهِ إِنَّ فِي ذَلِكَ لَآيَاتٍ لِّقَوْمٍ يَسْمَعُونَ {{الروم/23}

---

114. **[28:20]** And a man came from the farthest end of the city, running. He said, "O Moses, indeed the eminent ones are conferring over you [intending] to kill you, so leave [the city]; indeed, I am to you of the sincere advisors."
[28:21] So he left it, fearful and anticipating [apprehension]. He said, "My Lord, save me from the wrongdoing people."
115. And of His signs is your sleep by night and day and your seeking of His bounty. Indeed in that are signs for a people who listen.

One should remember that there are motivational milestones for each person.

There is a force that makes the person wake up in the morning to get dressed, to eat and to have joy in his or her engagement.

This force is called motivational milestone for each person.

This motivational milestone can be the fear of not fulfilling a responsibility. A responsibility at work, a responsibility related with the children or a responsibility being at the college or school.

This motivational milestone can be making another day with earning further, investing in business and engaging with achievements or gains.

This motivational milestone for a person of Allah ﷻ can be another great day to appreciate and thank what Allah ﷻ has given to this person by using the time to seek for opportunities increasing one's knowledge of Allah ﷻ, marifatullah, and to invite others to the path of Allah ﷻ. For the true person of imān, these two engagements are very attractive, motivating and joyful.

There is another category that they don't really realize each day as an opportunity and responsibility. They have the attitudes and approaches of "again, it is another boring day." This category can include immature children or youth. Or, it can include the people who have pessimistic perspectives of life without much meaning and purpose.

A person of imān should realize that although his inner-self is only and truly satisfied with marifatullah and sharing this with others, he or she can swing at other motivational milestones when wandering around. In other words, the society and our own ego-nafs may pull us to other motivational milestones and we can find ourselves in those valleys.

Yet, it is expected that the real person of imān sees the temporal feature of other milestones and realize and appreciate the real and permanent motivational milestones with the perspectives of marifatullah and sharing it with others.

اَللّٰهُمَّ جَعَلْنَا مَنْ اِتّبع الحقَ، آمِيْن

Allahumma Ja'alna man attabil'al Haqq, Amìn

اَللّٰهُمَّ صَلِّ عَلَى سَيِّدِنَا وَمَولَانا حَبِيْبَنَا مُحَمَّد ﷺ

Allahumma Salli Ala Sayyidina wa Mawlana wa Habibina Muhammad ﷺ

Juz 24

Sûrah 39 al-Zumar

[54]¹¹⁶

Past Engagements with Guilt, Future Expectations with Wahm, and the Need to Focus on the Present

قُلْ يَا عِبَادِيَ الَّذِينَ أَسْرَفُوا عَلَى أَنفُسِهِمْ لَا تَقْنَطُوا مِن رَّحْمَةِ اللَّهِ إِنَّ اللَّهَ يَغْفِرُ الذُّنُوبَ جَمِيعًا إِنَّهُ هُوَ الْغَفُورُ الرَّحِيمُ {الزمر/ 53} وَأَنِيبُوا إِلَى رَبِّكُمْ وَأَسْلِمُوا لَهُ مِن قَبْلِ أَن يَأْتِيَكُمُ الْعَذَابُ ثُمَّ لَا تُنصَرُونَ {الزمر/ 54}

قَالَ وَمَن يَقْنَطُ مِن رَّحْمَةِ رَبِّهِ إِلاَّ الضَّالُّونَ {الحجر/ 56}¹¹⁷

One should remember that past engagements are gone. If a person thinks the problems of these engagements, now it doesn't exist one should make shukr to Allah ﷻ. If a person thinks the n'imahs of these engagements, then one should make shukr to Allah ﷻ that if it has a real value that can really benefit the person in afterlife.

One should remember that our present time that we are in, needs the most focus. The finished past and unknown future can be used for motivational purposes in one's life.

One can think about one's past with its mistakes, sins, errors and problems and make constant tawbah to Allah ﷻ and asking Allah ﷻ removing the evil effects of this past on the present time, future and afterlife.

One can think about future to motivate oneself to please Allah ﷻ with a real purpose and goal. This motivation is called fruitful intention. Even, the person may not have the means and time to achieve, Allah ﷻ may still give him or her the rewards of this real and fruitful intention.

Both past and future have important roles in one's life. Past requires tawbah and shukr and hamd for Allah ﷻ. Future requires protection and

---

116. **[39:53]** Say, "O My servants who have transgressed against themselves [by sinning], do not despair of the mercy of Allah. Indeed, Allah forgives all sins. Indeed, it is He who is the Forgiving, the Merciful." **[39:54]** And return [in repentance] to your Lord and submit to Him before the punishment comes upon you; then you will not be helped.

117. He said, "And who despairs of the mercy of his Lord except for those astray?"

asking openings of blessings from Allah ﷻ. Present is the meeting place of both past and future.

For the past memories of the person, sometimes a negative feeling of guilt disconnected from Allah ﷻ with the absence of tawbah in the present time can serve to destroy the person spiritually with pessimism at the present time as mentioned[118] قَالَ وَمَن يَقْنَطُ مِن رَّحْمَةِ رَبِّهِ إِلَّا الضَّالُّونَ {الحجر/65}

Guilt without tawbah destroys the person.

On a positive note, the real position of a person of imān is mentioned[119] قُلْ يَا عِبَادِيَ الَّذِينَ أَسْرَفُوا عَلَى أَنفُسِهِمْ لَا تَقْنَطُوا مِن رَّحْمَةِ اللَّهِ إِنَّ اللَّهَ يَغْفِرُ الذُّنُوبَ جَمِيعًا as إِنَّهُ هُوَ الْغَفُورُ الرَّحِيمُ {الزمر/53} وَأَنِيبُوا إِلَى رَبِّكُمْ وَأَسْلِمُوا لَهُ مِن قَبْلِ أَن يَأْتِيَكُمُ الْعَذَابُ ثُمَّ لَا تُنصَرُونَ {الزمر/54}

Sometimes, a positive memory of the past can distract the person to focus on the present. One should remember that thinking about the good and virtuous days in the past can give a pleasure to the person. Yet, this memory related pleasure in its reality is not for this life but for afterlife as mentioned in the conversations of afterlife as قَالَ قَائِلٌ مِّنْهُمْ إِنِّي كَانَ لِي قَرِينٌ {الصافات/51}. Sometimes, we call this type of people as the people "living in the past." Then, we remind this person to come to the present.

Sometimes, expectations of future can disconnect the person from the present and make him or her not appreciate what he or she has at the present time. The unrealistic expectations are referred as wahm-illusions.

Yet, the increase of n'imahs in the future require the focus of the present with shukr and hamd as mentioned وَإِذْ تَأَذَّنَ رَبُّكُمْ لَئِن شَكَرْتُمْ لَأَزِيدَنَّكُمْ وَلَئِن كَفَرْتُمْ إِنَّ عَذَابِي لَشَدِيدٌ {إبراهيم/7}

There is nothing wrong to have a goal and real intention to work towards. In fact, everyone should have this real intention. The real intention is to please Allah ﷻ. Yet, present is the time that we are in. Present needs our focus for decision making and execution of the actions to achieve our real intention and goal.

---

118. He said, "And who despairs of the mercy of his Lord except for those astray?"
119. **[39:53]** Say, "O My servants who have transgressed against themselves [by sinning], do not despair of the mercy of Allah. Indeed, Allah forgives all sins. Indeed, it is He who is the Forgiving, the Merciful." **[39:54]** And return [in repentance] to your Lord and submit to Him before the punishment comes upon you; then you will not be helped.

In all of these classifications, one should remember that past, present and future are all human and creation related renderings.

Allah ﷻ is al-Awwal, al-Akhir, and al-Haqq.

Making dua to Allah ﷻ for forgiveness, tawbah, help, 'iana, openings, and blessings is the key of everything. With this enablement and empowerment received from Allah ﷻ with the Divine Grace, Fadl, Karam, then one should move on in the journeys of time in one's limited life in this dunya towards to results of this journey in the afterlife.

May Allah ﷻ protect us from the evil effects of our sins in the past, present and future.

May Allah ﷻ lift us with the Divine Grace and Fadl and Karam with all due to the Habìb ﷺ

اَللّٰهُمَّ صَلِّ عَلَى سَيِّدِنَا مُحَمَّد ﷺ الحبيب ﷺ

Allahumma Salli ala Sayyidina Muhammad ﷺ al-Habìb ﷺ

Handling the Problems of the Present

One should remember that the degree of the effect of a present problem can decrease if the person welcomes the problem, accepts it, and take it easy.

In other a person can take all the preventative measures with caution and alertness to prevent emerging of a problem.

Yet, when it emerges and displays, the person should be in a welcoming mode of a guest compared to his or her preventative mode of alertness that may somehow also indicate tension. The imbalance or extreme forms of tension is panic, horror and terrifying states of heart and mind.

If the person is in the problem at a present time, the attitude and embodiment of "welcoming the guest" as a visitor coming from Allah ﷻ can make the person relax, accept and benefit and learn from this problem.

Yes, every incident in one's life is a guest sent by Allah ﷻ to teach us and remind us something on the path of our struggle for Allah ﷻ.

One should remember that the person should differentiate the stage of a problem. If it was in the past, if is still in the present or if it is expected in the future.

For the problems of the past that the person still feels and thinks that it is affecting his or her current time, is explained in the above section with the concepts of positive and negative guilt.

If the problem is not present but to come from future, then the person can take all the precautions to prevent it.

If it already emerged and the person is in the problem at the present time, then taking it easy and welcoming it and learning from this experience is important.

An example can be that a person who is dealing with a naughty child with tantrums with seriousness can actually increase the results of the problems.

Yet, a person who is dealing with the same child laughing or smiling for his tantrums and trying to learn from this child's behavior can actually minimize the conflicts and transform an outward unpleasant experience to a pleasant memory of a learning opportunity for oneself. Here, we are focusing on the effects of this analysis on oneself, if even one considers the effect of this attitude on the child, this attitude of easiness can also have positive effect on the child compared to the seriousness of the person taking some serious measures of lecturing or putting the child in time out.

One day, the Prophet ﷺ was joking with a child who had a bird as a pet. The Prophet ﷺ was still smiling, joking and accepting the child's tantrums instead of lecturing him. It is interesting that the scholars of legal rulings deduced around 350 legal rulings only from this interaction of the Prophet ﷺ with this child.

The way of handling problem solving or handling the problems at the present time aim to minimize the spiritual scars. Problems solving is not a math problem that has one-to-one correspondence as today's behavioral psychology or conflict resolutions approaches can propose.

One always relocates and re-centers oneself in one's intention with Allah ﷻ if he or she is facing a problem at a present time. Accordingly, moving forward by taking it easy on the problem is critical especially when the problems are all around peripheral parts of one's main intention with imān, ihsān and Islām.

This spiritual alignment or re-centering oneself evolves around the main intention of pleasing Allah ﷻ in decision making and taking an action that would be affecting a person's life and afterlife. In this regard, one of the ways of problem solving indicates leaving a minimum spiritual scar and damage on the involved parties.

To understand this better, one should know that backbiting (giybah) is considered to be worse than adultery as mentioned by Rasulullah ﷺ. This is just one example of minimizing the spiritual scars on people in social, family or professional related engagements.

اَللهُمَّ يَسِّر ولاتُعَسِّر وَتَمِّم بِلْخَيْر

اَللهُمَّ صَلِّ عَلَى سَيِّدِنَا مُحَمّد ﷺ

Allahumma Yassir wa La tu'assir wa tammim bil-Khayr
Allahumma Salli Ala Sayyidina Muhammad ﷺ

[54-59][120]

The Case of the Serial Killer, Throwing Oneself Forward, and Turning to Allah ﷻ

قُلْ يَا عِبَادِيَ الَّذِينَ أَسْرَفُوا عَلَى أَنفُسِهِمْ لَا تَقْنَطُوا مِن رَّحْمَةِ اللَّهِ إِنَّ اللَّهَ يَغْفِرُ الذُّنُوبَ جَمِيعًا إِنَّهُ هُوَ الْغَفُورُ الرَّحِيمُ {الزمر/35} وَأَنِيبُوا إِلَى رَبِّكُمْ وَأَسْلِمُوا لَهُ مِن قَبْلِ أَن يَأْتِيَكُمُ الْعَذَابُ ثُمَّ لَا تُنصَرُونَ {الزمر/45} وَاتَّبِعُوا أَحْسَنَ مَا أُنزِلَ إِلَيْكُم مِّن رَّبِّكُم مِّن قَبْلِ أَن يَأْتِيَكُمُ العَذَابُ بَغْتَةً وَأَنتُمْ لَا تَشْعُرُونَ {الزمر/55} أَن تَقُولَ نَفْسٌ يَا حَسْرَتَى عَلَى مَا فَرَّطتُ فِي جَنبِ اللَّهِ وَإِن كُنتُ لَمِنَ السَّاخِرِينَ {الزمر/65}

أَوْ تَقُولَ لَوْ أَنَّ اللَّهَ هَدَانِي لَكُنتُ مِنَ الْمُتَّقِينَ {الزمر/57} أَوْ تَقُولَ حِينَ تَرَى الْعَذَابَ لَوْ أَنَّ لِي كَرَّةً فَأَكُونَ مِنَ الْمُحْسِنِينَ {الزمر/58} بَلَى قَدْ جَاءتْكَ آيَاتِي فَكَذَّبْتَ بِهَا وَاسْتَكْبَرْتَ وَكُنتَ مِنَ الْكَافِرِينَ {الزمر/59}

One should remember that our needs are endless. We have our weak moments trying to destroy us. Yet, dua and struggling as much as possible to die on the path of Allah ﷻ is very critical. In this struggle,

---

120. **53.**Say, "O My servants who have transgressed against themselves [by sinning], do not despair of the mercy of Allah. Indeed, Allah forgives all sins. Indeed, it is He who is the Forgiving, the Merciful."**54.** And return [in repentance] to your Lord and submit to Him before the punishment comes upon you; then you will not be helped.
55. And follow the best of what was revealed to you from your Lord [i.e., the Qurān] before the punishment comes upon you suddenly while you do not perceive, **56.** Lest a soul should say, "Oh, [how great is] my regret over
what I neglected in regard to Allah and that I was among the mockers."**57.** Or [lest] it say, "If only Allah had guided me, I would have been among the righteous."**58.** Or [lest] it say when it sees the punishment, "If only I had another turn so I could be among the doers of good."**59.** But yes, there had come to you My verses, but you denied them
and were arrogant, and you were among the disbelievers.

one should always remember the hadith of the serial killer who killed one hundred people [20]. On the way for his struggle to be on the path of Allah ﷻ, he throws his body forward to be close to the path that he is going for. One can remember the incident of above ayahs with the case Wahshi (رضي الله عنه) when he (رضي الله عنه) killed Hamza (رضي الله عنه) at the times of Jahiliyyah. He (رضي الله عنه) was also looking the means to turn to Allah ﷻ. Rasulullah ﷺ invited him by sending the set of Wahshi (رضي الله عنه).

This reminds us two critical points. One is that we should have a goal and purpose on the path of Allah ﷻ, then go for it and struggle as much as possible. The second one is that this struggle should not consider or prevented by any of the human valuation systems. In this case of the person, pushing himself forward and throwing himself towards the direction of his destination may not have much possible meaning for humans. Yet, this last push may have a huge value for Allah ﷻ to indicate a projection of the person if he lived longer what he would do. SubhanAllah!

Another is the story of an ant going to pilgrimage can be a key in this regard to emphasize our intention until we die.

أَللَّهُمَّ صَلِّ عَلَى سَيِّدِنَا وحبيبنا مُحَمَّد ﷺ

Allahumma Salli Ala Sayyidina wa Habibina Muhammad ﷺ.

Self-Blame & Guilt

One should remember that Allah ﷻ can help the person remove all the burdens overwhelming his or her heart and mind.

Sometimes, our inability of not controlling ourselves induces us with destructive self-blame of guilt. The reality can be that we could have made a mistake although we have been watching ourselves and preparing ourselves not to fall into the same trap over and over.

Yet, our spiritual messiness being induced at all times can overtake our willpower and leave us again in destructions of self-blame or guilt.

At all times, the person cannot lose hope from Allah ﷻ.

At this time of the dare need of the person for Allah ﷻ, the person can open his or her hands to Allah ﷻ discharge and empty oneself with crying, and help.

Sometimes, a person with overconfidence can make a lot of mistakes.

Sometimes, a person with nonconfidence can make less mistakes.

Yet, our confidence always related with Allah ﷻ but not on ourselves.

We ask Allah ﷻ to give us the iradah-will power to act and execute properly in the world of causalities and beyond by fully having full Trust-Tawakkul to Allah ﷻ, Amìn.

May Allah ﷻ make us act and execute to please Allah ﷻ on the path, Amìn

Juz 25

Sûrah 41 Fussilat

Emotions, Reason, Istiqamah & Istigfar

قُلْ إِنَّمَا أَنَا بَشَرٌ مِّثْلُكُمْ يُوحَى إِلَيَّ أَنَّمَا إِلَهُكُمْ إِلَهٌ وَاحِدٌ فَاسْتَقِيمُوا إِلَيْهِ وَاسْتَغْفِرُوهُ وَوَيْلٌ لِّلْمُشْرِكِينَ {فصلت/6} 121

One should remember we are constantly challenged by our emotions and reason in decision making in order to establish istiqāmah.

One should remember that istiqāmah is achieved with istighfār.

One should remember that Allah ﷻ constantly showers the Divine ni'mahs-bounties on us. Our emotions constantly want to rule against but not for the best interest of the person.

Emotions want care, love, and recognition.

Reasons try to foresee the benefits and interests.

It is extremely difficult to balance both. SubhanAllah!

Sometimes, the reason and intellect of the person see a benefit in an engagement.

Yet, emotions can be so overwhelming that although the person may see the benefit, he or she may not engage with this action.

In this case, we critically focus the notions of mayl-inclinations forming our decision making and execution of our actions.

The key question is "how do we activate our inclinations-mayl that is going to make us sound decisions leading to sound actions?"

---

121. Say, O [Muhammad], "I am only a man like you to whom it has been revealed that your god is but one God; so take a straight course to Him and seek His forgiveness." And woe to those who associate others with Allah -

The scholarship especially focuses on the importance of personal spiritual care through awrad-wird/spiritual practices that would make the person keep going similar to a gas in the car.

Even, there can be an excellent car like Tesla or Ferrari, if there is power either through gas or electric nowadays, then there won't be any movement.

One can also take this discussion with the concepts of free-will, inclination and decision making. Then, action occurs.

One of the basic and simply looking spiritual care practice is the embodiment of acceptance of the person's position in front of Allah ﷻ, Rabbul A'lamin.

The acceptance of this position can be referred as "istighfār" with the term "astagfirullah." Or, this can be expressed with "la hawla wa la quwwata illa billah"

The acceptance of one's position with the embodiment of simply looking above two phrases can actually transform the person with power.

One should remember our struggle between our mind and emotions is to achieve istiqāmah to please Allah ﷻ. One of the key ingredients of istiqamah is istighfār.

أللهم جَعَلنا مِنهُم ،آمين

Allahumma Ja'alna Minhum

أللهُمَّ صَلِّ عَلَى سَيِّدِنَا وحبيبِنا مُحَمّد ﷺ وعلى آله اجمعين

Allahumma Salli a'la Sayyidina wa Habibina Muhammad ﷺ wa a'la alihi ajmā'in.

Sûrah 42 al-shûrã

[23][122]

ذَلِكَ الَّذِي يُبَشِّرُ اللَّهُ عِبَادَهُ الَّذِينَ آمَنُوا وَعَمِلُوا الصَّالِحَاتِ قُل لَّا أَسْأَلُكُمْ عَلَيْهِ أَجْرًا إِلَّا الْمَوَدَّةَ فِي الْقُرْبَى وَمَن يَقْتَرِفْ حَسَنَةً نَزِدْ لَهُ فِيهَا حُسْنًا إِنَّ اللَّهَ غَفُورٌ شَكُورٌ {{الشورى/23}}

Not Following the Sunnah of Rasulullah ﷺ is an Ingratitude to Rasulullah ﷺ

---

122. It is that of which Allah gives good tidings to His servants who believe and do righteous deeds. Say, [O Muhammad], "I do not ask you for this message any payment [but] only good will through kinship." And whoever commits a good deed - We will increase for him good therein. Indeed, Allah is Forgiving and Appreciative.

One should remember that Rasulullah ﷺ had the utmost concern of this ummah. His specific ummah includes all the people from his time of nubuwwah until End of Days. His general ummah includes all the humanity as Rasulullah was sent as Rahmatan LilA'lamìn for all mankind as mentioned[123] {الأنبياء/107} وَمَا أَرْسَلْنَاكَ إِلاَّ رَحْمَةً لِّلْعَالَمِينَ

And also, Rasulullah has the position of the lead of all the anbiyā which indicates that the general in chief can have authority and responsibility for each specific groups of generals leading their group similar to the anbiyā (عليهم السلام).

It is narrated in the books by the people of kashf (inner sciences) that at his blessed birth ﷺ, Rasulullah ﷺ uttered the words as "ummatì, ummatì, ummatì" showing his ﷺ utmost concern for his people until the End of Days and all humanity in general.

As also it is an authentic hadith in multiple narrations of different books that in the Day of Judgment, when everyone is running to save their own selves; a mother doesn't care about her newborn as the ayah mentions; a friend doesn't care about his closest buddy; and even prophets do focus about the concerns if they displeased Allah ﷻ; then the only person who emerges in singularity, uniqueness and distinctiveness is Rasulullah ﷺ. Rasulullah ﷺ again utters the same words at this time similar to his blessed birth ﷺ with full embodiment as "ummatì, ummatì, ummatì."

Now, one can ask, "how useless and lowly is the person who belittles the sunnah of Rasulullah ﷺ and expects benefit from Rasulullah ﷺ in the afterlife when there is full complete and absolute fear and anguish due to Azamah of Allah ﷻ and the Judment Day in front of Rabbul A'lamìn ﷻ ?"

Yet, Rasulullah ﷺ is the person of embodiment of ihsān which means that Rasulullah ﷺ does not correspond people as us. In other words, Rasulullah ﷺ gives the one who doesn't give back. Rasulullah ﷺ helps the person who doesn't help. Rasulullah ﷺ forgives the person who comes to kill Rasulullah ﷺ as mentioned in different narrations in his blessed life ﷺ.

Yet, lowly and unfortunate is the person who claims to be Muslim and belittles the sunnah of Rasulullah ﷺ with actions, words and by not giving importance to follow it.

---

123. And We have not sent you, [O Muhammad], except as a mercy to the worlds.

May Allah ﷻ protect us, Amìn.

Humans are generally motivated on interest-based relationships. Shouldn't this unfortunate human at least try to follow the sunnah of Rasulullah and accordingly expect some help in this life and afterlife?

SubhanAllah! Unfortunate are the ones who claim to be a Muslim but yet, not being grateful to Rasulullah ﷺ about how much he ﷺ did for us and expected to do much more for us in the afterlife inshAllah.

May Allah ﷻ protect us to be ungrateful to Rasulullah ﷺ by not following his sunnah ﷺ, Amìn.

اَللّٰهُمَّ صَلِّ عَلَى سَيِّدِنَا وَ حَبِيْبِنَا وَ إِمَامَنَا وَمَوْلَانَا مُحَمَّد المصطفى المحسن ﷺ

Allahumma ala Sayyidina wa Habìbina Imāmana Mawlana Muhammad al-Mustafa al-Muhsin ﷺ, Amìn.

The Love for Ahlu-Bayt

One should remember that the constant emphasis of love for the family and descendants of Rasulullah ﷺ is not only a mere love without any purpose, hikmah-wisom, and reason.

Yes, our primary love stems due to the love of the ones because of the Loved One. We love Rasulullah ﷺ because he ﷺ is al-Habìb al-Mutlak ﷺ , the absolute loved one ﷺ by Allah ﷻ.

Similarly, we love ahlu-bayt due al-Habìb ﷺ.

This is our initial primary position.

Now, for the hikmah and wisdom related renderings, let's analyze a few points.

There is always hikmah and wisdom behind this love as emphasized by Rasulullah ﷺ.

When we analyze the blessed life of Rasulullah ﷺ, there are narrations that depict the love of Rasulullah ﷺ in the blessed masjid Nabawiyy as for example Rasulullah ﷺ kissing Hasan (رضي الله عنه) and Husayn (رضي الله عنه), and publicizing his love ﷺ often in public among the sahabah and for the generations that would come later.

Yes, this publicity is not only mere human side of Rasulullah ﷺ but one of the hikmahs is that to tell the ummah that his blessed offspring ﷺ has a mission and responsibility of carrying the blessed mission of teachings of nubuwwah after Rasulullah ﷺ.

One should remember that there is no prophet and anbiya after Rasulullah ﷺ. Yet, ahlu-bayt has a natural and fitrì disposition of carrying the mission of nubuwwah after Rasulullah ﷺ.

When we review the ayahs of the Qurān and analyze the content of the salawāt, one can realize that this was also the reality for Ibrahim as mentioned[124] وَوَهَبْنَا لَهُ إِسْحَقَ وَيَعْقُوبَ وَجَعَلْنَا فِي ذُرِّيَّتِهِ النُّبُوَّةَ وَالْكِتَابَ وَآتَيْنَاهُ أَجْرَهُ فِي الدُّنْيَا وَإِنَّهُ فِي الْآخِرَةِ لَمِنَ الصَّالِحِينَ {العنكبوت/27}

Ibrahim as explicitly made dua to Allah ﷻ to have his offsprings and descendants to carry the mission of risalah after him as mentioned[125] وَإِذِ ابْتَلَى إِبْرَاهِيمَ رَبُّهُ بِكَلِمَاتٍ فَأَتَمَّهُنَّ قَالَ إِنِّي جَاعِلُكَ لِلنَّاسِ إِمَامًا قَالَ وَمِن ذُرِّيَّتِي قَالَ لاَ يَنَالُ عَهْدِي الظَّالِمِينَ {البقرة/124}. Then, as his dua was accepted, there were numerous prophets sent from the offspring and descendants of Ibrahim as.

In this sense, if we analyze the As-salawatu Ibrahimiyyah as the highest level of salawat as mentioned by Rasulullah 9] [10] ﷺ] that we read in our salah as:

أَللهُمَّ صَلِّ /بَارِك على سَيِّدَنا مُحَمَّد كَمَا صَلَّيْتَ على سَيِّدنا إبراهيم و على آل سيدنا إبراهيم إنك حميد مجيد

Allahumma salli/barik a'lā sayyidina Muhammad wa a'lā āli Sayyidina Muhammad kama sallayta a'lā sayyidina Ibrahìm wa a'lā a'li Sayyidina Ibrahim Innaka Hamìdun Majid.

One can realize that a'li Sayydina Ibrahim is the all the anbiya in its immediate meaning who took the message of nubuwwah after Ibrahim as.

Similarly, a'lā āli Sayyidina Muhammad are all the ahlu-bayt off springs of Rasulullah ﷺ in its immediate meaning who took the message of nubuwwah after Ibrahim as. As mentioned there is no prophet and anbiya after Rasulullah ﷺ. Yet, ahlu-bayt has a natural and fitrì disposition of carrying the mission of nubuwwah after Rasulullah ﷺ.

This is does not mean that the value of people in Islām is due to the offspring or descendant relation. No, the level of the person with Allah

---

124. And We gave to Him Isaac and Jacob and placed in his descendants prophethood and scripture. And We gave him his reward in this world, and indeed, he is in the Hereafter among the righteous.

125. And [mention, O Muhammad], when Abraham was tried by his Lord with commands and he fulfilled them. [Allah] said, "Indeed, I will make you a leader for the people." [Abraham] said, "And of my descendants?" [Allah] said, "My covenant does not include the wrongdoers."

⁕ is with their taqwa regardless of their descendancy as mentioned[126] إِنَّ اَكْرَمَكُمْ عِندَ اللهِ أَتْقَاكُمْ إِنَّ اللهَ عَلِيمٌ خَبِيرٌ {الحجرات/13}

To emphasize this point, Rasulullah ⁕ made and certain people to be from the ahlu-bayt although they didn't have seeming biological relationship with Rasulullah ⁕. For example, Rasulullah ⁕ said "Salman is from ahlu-bayt," [23] although Salman ra was originally farisi-persian and migrated to Medina from thousands of miles, SubhanAllah!

One can even see the opposite case of this point for the biological son of Nûh as. When Nûh as said "my son is from my ahl-family" Allah ⁕ revealed an ayah and mentioned that was not the case as mentioned[127] وَنَادَى نُوحٌ رَّبَّهُ فَقَالَ رَبِّ إِنَّ ابْنِي مِنْ أَهْلِي وَإِنَّ وَعْدَكَ الْحَقُّ وَأَنتَ أَحْكَمُ الْحَاكِمِينَ {هود/45}

قَالَ يَا نُوحُ إِنَّهُ لَيْسَ مِنْ أَهْلِكَ إِنَّهُ عَمَلٌ غَيْرُ صَالِحٍ فَلَا تَسْأَلْنِ مَا لَيْسَ لَكَ بِهِ عِلْمٌ إِنِّي أَعِظُكَ أَن تَكُونَ مِنَ الْجَاهِلِينَ {هود/46} قَالَ رَبِّ إِنِّي أَعُوذُ بِكَ أَنْ أَسْأَلَكَ مَا لَيْسَ لِي بِهِ عِلْمٌ وَإِلَّا تَغْفِرْ لِي وَتَرْحَمْنِي أَكُن مِّنَ الْخَاسِرِينَ {هود/47}

On the other hand, when review the giants-leads of Islām in history in the last 1500 years, in reality almost all of the pious salaf seem to have a lineage with Rasulullah ⁕ as the Ahlu-Bayt, SubhanAllah!

So, how do we understand this reality?

SubhanAllah, this can be one of the miracles of the Qurān and Rasulullah ⁕ besides many.

Allah ⁕ mentioned in the Qurān that there will not be any prophets after Rasulullah ⁕, his blessed offspring can be given this responsibility carrying the message similar to the offspring of Ibrahim as. Therefore, he ⁕ asked the love for his blessed offspring as the ahlu-bayt as mentioned[128] قُل لَّا أَسْأَلُكُمْ عَلَيْهِ أَجْرًا إِلَّا الْمَوَدَّةَ فِي الْقُرْبَى وَمَن يَقْتَرِفْ حَسَنَةً نَّزِدْ لَهُ فِيهَا حُسْنًا إِنَّ اللهَ غَفُورٌ شَكُورٌ {الشورى/23}

---

126. O mankind, indeed We have created you from male and female and made you peoples and tribes that you may know one another. Indeed, the most noble of you in the sight of Allah is the most righteous of you. Indeed, Allah is Knowing and Acquainted.

127. **[11:45]** And Noah called to his Lord and said, "My Lord, indeed my son is of my family; and indeed, Your promise is true; and You are the most just of judges!" **[11:46]** He said, "O Noah, indeed he is not of your family; indeed, he is [one whose] work was other than righteous, so ask Me not for that about which you have no knowledge. Indeed, I advise you, lest you be among the ignorant." **[11:47]** [Noah] said, "My Lord, I seek refuge in You from asking that of which I have no knowledge. And unless You forgive me and have mercy upon me, I will be among the losers."

128. "I do not ask you for this message any payment [but] only good will through kinship." And whoever commits a good deed - We will increase for him good therein. Indeed, Allah is Forgiving and Appreciative.

He 🕊 possibly realized that as generations grow the number of his offspring would increase but yet, at the same time, the qualitative strength of Muslims will decrease although Muslims can be many in number.

At these Dajjalic times, where a lot of confusion and lies as truths are presented, the critical point of following a Jam'ah is emphasized by Rasulullah 🕊 by indicating that forming and making Ja'maah around the people of ahlu-bayt.

One should remember there are two types of imān and following. One is with the mind, intelellect, and constant struggle of convincing against the doubts and the other is following due to the identity or belonging. This type of imān can have praiseworthy perspectives.

Although some of the ahlu-bayt may not have mind related following of Islām, the natural-fitri embeded of their position as a Muslim can make their submission at a higher level for the Divine teachings at the times of confusion of Dajjalic era where everyone tries to use their mind to be convinced and a lot of demagocy is presented with lies covering up the truth.

At these times, the people of ahlu-bayt can be the sincere fitri people of identity following the Divine teachings of Allah 🕊 and Rasulullah 🕊 as a clear guidance.

On a negative note, a person of blind follower may not leave a bātil due to their natural identity belonging.

How about a person who is really following the Haqq-the Obvious and Clear Truth, the teachings of Islām as the teachings of the Qurān and Rasulullah 🕊 ? Would he leave these teachings? The answer is definitely No. This is position of ahlu-bayt.

SubhanAllah!

One should always remember in above discussions the definition of true ahlu-bayt. In one of the hadith, Rasulullah 🕊 mentions that "I leave you after me two things. If you follow them, then you would be saved. Ones is Kitabullah and the other is my ahlu-bayt," [11]. When this hadith is combined with other ahadith of Rasulullah 🕊, then the scholars unanimously interpret at the level of Ijma that "ahlu-bayt" in the above hadith represents Sunnah of Rasulullah 🕊 and all the applications and teachings of hādith. A person is not really considered ahlu-bayt if he or she does not follow and value Rasulullah 🕊, the teachings of Rasulullah 🕊, sunnah and hadith of Rasulullah 🕊, the ones who are loved by Rasulullah ﷺ such as the sahabah who carried us the knowledge of hadith and sunnahs of Rasulullah ﷺ to us.

One should know that at the time of Rasulullah ﷺ, all the immediate ahlu-bayt, Ali (رضي الله عنه), Fatima (رضي الله عنها), Hasan (رضي الله عنه), Husayin (رضي الله عنه) were all utmost humble but did not claim any superiority due to their descendent proximity to Rasulullah ﷺ. Yet, the sahabah (رضي الله عنهم اجمعين) treated them with utmost respect and honor and care. SubhanAllah! This is the lost relationship unfortunately.

In other words, a true sign of true ahlu-bayt is the follower of sunnah of Rasulullah ﷺ. Most of the giant salaf has the biological descendency of lineage with Rasulullah ﷺ. All the people of Allah ﷻ as ahlulullah has the potential of being ahlu-bayt regardless of their biological relationship with Rasulullah ﷺ or not as in the case of Salman ra, as in the opposite cases of son of Nuh as and uncle of Rasulullah ﷺ, Abu-Lahab.

May Allah ﷻ protect us from misguidance and make us follow the teachings of the Qurān and Sunnah of Rasulullah ﷺ, Amìn.

May Allah ﷻ give us the love for the Ahlu-Bayt.

أَللّٰهُمَّ صَلِّ وبَارِك على سَيِّدَنا مُحَمَّد كَمَا صَلَّيْتَ على سَيِّدِنا إبراهيم وعلى آل سيدنا إبراهيم إنك حميد مجيد

Allahumma salli/barik a'lā sayyidina Muhammad wa a'lā āli Sayyidina Muhammad kama sallayta a'lā sayyidina Ibrahìm wa a'lā a'li Sayyidina Ibrahim Innaka Hamìdun Majìd.

Sûrah 43 al-Zukhruf

وَمَن يَعْشُ عَن ذِكْرِ الرَّحْمَنِ نُقَيِّضْ لَهُ شَيْطَانًا فَهُوَ لَهُ قَرِينٌ {36/الزخرف}129

Wird/Awrad: Regular Rituals of Connection with Allah ﷻ

One should remember that Allah ﷻ can do anything at any time beyond the causalities. Yet, our hearts and mind constantly yearn and desire for Allah ﷻ on the path with the right ingredients of spritual food and drink.

Sometimes, a person who is hungry rushes to eat snack and fast food. Yet, although in its immediate feelings, he or she feels good, but

---

129. And whoever is blinded from remembrance of the Most Merciful - We appoint for him a devil, and he is to him a companion.

after a few minutes, he or she may curse to oneself as "why did I eat this? My stomach hurts."

Feeling our need for Allah ﷻ is the first step and that is very noble.

Yet, giving the right food and drink is the key.

In this sense, when we talk about spiritual practice, the notions of awrad, wird, teacher, Shayqh, murabbi, a good friend are all terms to indicate a type of rich nutrient spiritual feast with a good plan of nutritionist.

May Allah ﷻ help us to be patient on the path with the right choice, Amìn.

Allahumma Salli A'la Sayyidina Muhammad ﷺ.

One should remember that the person should always attach one's heart on the path of Allah ﷻ.

Sometimes, due to wrong good seeming thoughts, inclinations, decisions or actions, the person can receive some Divine Gentle warnings to align the position of the person on the path of Allah ﷻ.

May Allah ﷻ give us istiqamah

لاحول ولاقوة الا بالله

La Hawla wa la Quwwata illa Billah

أَللهُمَّ صَلِّ على سَيِّدَنا مُحَمَّد ﷺ

Allahumma Salli A'la Sayyidina Muhammad ﷺ

Juz 26

Sûrah 46 al-Jāthiyah

[14]¹³⁰

Goal and Purpose in Life & Days of Allah ﷻ

قُل لِّلَّذِينَ آمَنُوا يَغْفِرُوا لِلَّذِينَ لا يَرْجُونَ أَيَّامَ اللهِ لِيَجْزِيَ قَوْمًا بِما كَانُوا يَكْسِبُونَ
{{14/الجاثية}}

One should know that Allah ﷻ is al-Qādir. Allah ﷻ can do anything at any time. Our inability to constantly connect Allah ﷻ with Dhikr and remembrance of Allah ﷻ sometimes make us wander around emotionally and mentally.

---

130. Say, [O Muhammad], to those who have believed that they [should] forgive those who expect not the days of Allah so that He may recompense a people for what they used to earn.

Yet, in all these wanderings without the sufficient amount of remembrance of Allah ﷻ or Dhikrullah can put the person in false and depressive states of heart and mind.

At these times and all the times, one should always connect to Allah ﷻ with Dhikrullah and shatter the gloomy perspectives of pessimism, purposelessness and meaninglessness around oneself.

One should remember that a nice sunny day will not last long. There will be the night at the end. There will be the cold. There will be the dark weather with fog.

In all different days of Allah ﷻ as ayyamullah mentioned أَيَّامَ اللهِ in the Qurān in the above ayah , one can only stabilize oneself being protected from the effects of the external changes is by connecting oneself very strongly to the Rope of Allah ﷻ that is the Qurān and sunnah of Rasulullah ﷺ.

Sometimes, a sunny day can be distracting that it can induce gaflah-heedless in one's relationship with Allah ﷻ. Yet, the person should always connect to Allah ﷻ with Dhikrullah at those times.

Mostly, a cold day with dark and foggy induce a state of emotional and mental chaos if the person does not have purpose in one's connection with Allah ﷻ.

In the places, like England and other parts of the world, one can find these external effects such as foggy or gloomy weathers often and common. Then, one can ask how can one in these external effects survive especially if the person is deprived of imān?

One should remember that Allah ﷻ gives everything for a purpose with hikmah-wisdom. Among them, one can find different spectrum of changes in one's life both through the external effects such as a weather change and internal changes such as evil-seeming incidents occurring in one's personal life.

In both, the hikmah-wisdom is to remind the person about the rush or fleeing to an exit point in order to get a purpose and meaning by connecting ourselves to Allah ﷻ with imān, and Dhikrullah and minimizing and eliminating the painful effect of these on our weak and vulnerable souls and hearts.

One should remember that Allah ﷻ is al-Hayy and al-Qayyum Who is Permanent but Not Changing and Not Being Affected.

In this regard, the only way to save oneself from the effects of these changing incidents is to connect to the One Who is al-Bāki, al-Hayy and al-Qayyum.

Yet, one can still find people who do not understand this reality from non-Muslims and who do not fully understand this reality from Muslims. Then, people with the absence of full understanding connect themselves to the changing things or purposes.

Any purpose other than Allah ﷻ is fake and pseudo. All these fake purposes and engagements can give immediate pain with stress and more pain in the long run with full regret.

Let's take the case of a hard worker person without imān and Dhikrullah. During my life as being a physicist, I used to observe the lives of some of the people who did not have imān and but used to be hard workers.

Some of the professors spent much time in different positions of being much busy: teaching, research, being a department chair, publishing a paper or a book, writing grants or advising PhD students.

As I had a good relationship with them, I used to visit them at their homes and check on them as they got older and retired.

It was unfortunate that when they retired from a busy life of much work, recognition and increased humanly disabilities of not able to drive to their offices made some of them miserable because of a lifelong occupation as a way of soothing their heart and mind. Yet, now, at the last few moments of remaining of their life, their purpose was not being accomplished.

Some had depression problems in their last moments. Some suffered further due to their loss in their immediate families giving them support.

Yes, the physical disabilities with the approach of death and old age is a reality without the choice of imān or not.

Yet, at these moments, for a person of imān, he or she can be more satisfied that one was constantly running behind for a goal and purpose with imān and now, they will meet with Allah ﷻ as they have been longing for this for along time.

On the other hand, a person of kufr can be in full shattered states of heart and mind along with his or her disabilities at the last moment of their death that what they ran behind was all temporary, useless without any purpose and they were all fake and illusionary, but not real. SubhanAllah!

One can now remember the last days of Rasulullah ﷺ. He ﷺ had the utmost difficulty of standing up to pray. Yet, people carried him ﷺ to continue to pray. In other words, Rasulullah ﷺ continued on the same path of goal, meaning and purpose until he ﷺ passed away. His last moments were joy of meeting with Allah ﷻ even he ﷺ was given the option by Allah ﷻ to live longer if he ﷺ had wanted [9], SubhanAllah!

Now, one can compare the case of Rasulullah ﷺ as a linear increase in one's purpose with a boost at the end of his blessed ﷺ demise compared to the cases of people such as the example of professors having the effects spiritual fall as if being sucked by black hole during their death.

One should remember that imān requires to detach oneself from everything except Allah ﷻ. La ilaha illa Allah is the reality either one chooses by choice and be happy. Or, one learns without choice at the end of this life as a late and missed opportunity with a full regret in the afterlife.

One of the requirements of imān is to share what we have as valuable and beneficial with others. In this regard, قُل لِّلَّذِينَ آمَنُوا يَغْفِرُوا لِلَّذِينَ لَا يَرْجُونَ أَيَّامَ اللَّهِ can also indicate the responsibility of sharing the pearl and diamond teachings of the Qurān and Sunnah of Rasulullah ﷺ with the ones who are in the shattered states of heart and mind due to the absence of the true imān giving all the creation their true purpose, meaning and hope in life.

May Allah ﷻ make us detach ourselves everything from our heart except La ilaha illa Allah Muhammadun Rasulullah ﷺ.

May Allah ﷻ protect us running behind false purposes and meanings other than Allah ﷻ and Rasulullah ﷺ.

Allahumma Salli ala Sayyidina wa Habibinā wa Mawlana Muhammad ﷺ.

When we analyze the above ayah[131] قُل لِّلَّذِينَ آمَنُوا يَغْفِرُوا لِلَّذِينَ لَا يَرْجُونَ أَيَّامَ اللَّهِ لِيَجْزِيَ قَوْمًا بِما كَانُوا يَكْسِبُونَ {الجاثية/41}, it is narrated by Ibn Abbas (رضي الله عنه) that when Allah ﷻ revealed an ayah "man yuqridullahi qardan hasana", a man from the ahlu-kitāb (yahudi) make fun of it. When Omar (رضي الله عنه) heart about this, he (رضي الله عنه) took his sword and set a mission to find this person. Then, Allah ﷻ revealed this ayah and Omar

131. Say, [O Muhammad], to those who have believed that they [should] forgive those who expect not the days of Allah so that He may recompense a people for what they used to earn.

(رضي الله عنه) stopped his mission (رضي الله عنه). This is mentioned in tafsir of Thalabi (rahimahullah) [3].

Sûrah 47 Muhammad

[19]¹³²

Testing Our Tawhid: Pure or Impure?

فَاعْلَمْ أَنَّهُ لَا إِلَهَ إِلَّا اللَّهُ وَاسْتَغْفِرْ لِذَنبِكَ وَلِلْمُؤْمِنِينَ وَالْمُؤْمِنَاتِ وَاللَّهُ يَعْلَمُ مُتَقَلَّبَكُمْ وَمَثْوَاكُمْ

{{محمد/19}}

One should know that Allah ﷻ is al-Sami' al-Basìr al-Bātin al-Zāhir and monitors constantly one's heart and mind.

It is important to detach from everything except Allah ﷻ in one's intention and efforts.

Humans are humans. They always leave us with frustrations not fulfilling our expectations.

I'badah and 'ubudiyyah to Allah ﷻ requires leaving everything fully and turning to only Allah fully.

This essence is called tawhid. This is the embodiment of La ilaha illa Allah.

Yet, one can ask do we really have tawhid in practices, emotions, expectations, thoughts and intentions?

When we expect something from others and be in frustrations, then this is opposite to La ilaha illa Allah.

Rasulullah ﷺ was journeying and has been journeying in different vertical states of tawhid, La ilaha illa Allah.

La ilaha illa Allah Muhammadan a'bduhu wa Rasuluhu is the approved state of u'budiyyah of Rasulullah ﷺ with full tawhid and full 'ubudiyyah –'ibadah to Allah ﷻ.

Yet, although we claim to say La ilaha illa Allah, our expectations with frustrations from others put us deviated from the reality of La ilaha illa Allah.

One can remember the incident of a person coming with a sword to kill Rasulullah ﷺ while he ﷺ was sleeping under the tree in an isolated

---

132. So know, [O Muhammad], that there is no deity except Allah and ask forgiveness for your sin and for the believing men and believing women. And Allah knows of your movement and your resting place.

place. When the man about to use his sword while standing against Rasulullah ﷺ resting under a tree [22], he calls Rasulullah ﷺ and says "who is going to save you from me oh Muhammad?" Rasulullah ﷺ answers the man with full embodiment of La ilaha illa Allah as "Allah!"

The Name of Allah ﷻ pronounced through the blessed body of Rasulullah makes the man drop his sword on the ground. Rasulullah ﷺ picks the sword and asks the same question to this man, then the man asks forgiveness. As a normal habit of Rasulullah ﷺ, he ﷺ forgives the man and the man with this incident embraces Islām.

The above example is not a simple issue of Rasulullah ﷺ calling Allah ﷻ in his answer to the man and the vibration or sounds or shocking sound make the man drop his sword.

One should know that if there was the entire army of the world and universe against Rasulullah ﷺ and came against him while he was unarmed in the sleeping position, and if the entire asked the same question, the same answer of Rasulullah ﷺ could have made all the mass destruction weapons annihilated. This is the true reality of La ilaha illa Allah.

Rasulullah ﷺ is at the highest maqām of embodiment of this reality.

اَللّٰهُمَّ صَلِّ على سَيِّدَنا مُحَمَّد ﷺ

Allahumma Salli ala Sayyidina Muhammad ﷺ

Alignment of the Heart and Mind

One should remember that one's life needs focus.

Focus occurs around La ilaha illa Allah Muhammadun Rasulullah ﷺ.

This focus is called alignment of the heart and mind as mentioned فَاعْلَمْ أَنَّهُ لَا إِلَهَ إِلَّا اللّٰهُ

Anything outside of this focus and not serving to this focus area called distractions, problems and disasters.

One should remember that personal calamities and disasters are called disasters if it defocuses the person's mind and heart from La ilaha illa Allah Muhammadun Rasulullah. If these evil-seeming incidents help the person to focus on La ilaha illa Allah Muhammadun Rasulullah ﷺ, then they are not called calamities but reminders, supporters, and technicians to make the alignment of heart and mind in tawhid.

Sometimes, we get pulled in different directions due to the responsibilities of life.

Yet, a person should constantly with determinism and effort should re-align and re-center oneself around La ilaha illa Allah Muhammadun Rasulullah ﷺ.

What does re-centering around La ilaha illa Allah Muhammdun Rasulullah ﷺ mean?

It means that if there are any life responsibilities and engagements that is not related or based on to serve La ilaha illa Allah Muhammadun Rasulullah, then it means that they are really not important.

The person should not really give much importance to it. If these engagements fail, it the person loose in these engagements, they have no or zero value. This should not be a source of stress, grief, and anxiety for the person.

One should prioritize the valuables in one's life. The first and only priority is La ilaha illa Allah Muhammadun Rasulullah ﷺ.

If others don't serve this only priority, then they are all distractions.

As machines need alignment, our hearts need alignment to center itself from its decentered position of La ilaha illa Allah Muhammadun Rasulullah ﷺ.

Five times prayers if done properly is sufficient to establish this alignment of the heart of the person.

Nawāfil, Sunnahs, and additional Dhikrullah fine tunes of this alignment for the heart and mind of the person.

أَللَّهُمَّ صَلِّ على سَيِّدَنا مولانا حبيبنا مُحَمَّد ﷺ

Allahumma Salli ala Sayyidina Mawlana Habibana Muhammad ﷺ.

[38]

Replacement of Groups & Deadly Group Identities

يَا أَيُّهَا الَّذِينَ آمَنُواْ مَا لَكُمْ إِذَا قِيلَ لَكُمُ انفِرُواْ فِي سَبِيلِ اللَّهِ اثَّاقَلْتُمْ إِلَى الأَرْضِ أَرَضِيتُم بِالْحَيَاةِ الدُّنْيَا مِنَ الآخِرَةِ فَمَا مَتَاعُ الْحَيَاةِ الدُّنْيَا فِي الآخِرَةِ إِلاَّ قَلِيلٌ {التوبة/38}¹³³ إِلاَّ

---

133. O you who have believed, what is [the matter] with you that, when you are told to go forth in the cause of Allah, you adhere heavily to the earth? Are you satisfied with the life of this world rather than the Hereafter? But what is the enjoyment of worldly life compared to the Hereafter except a [very] little.

تَنفِرُواْ يُعَذِّبْكُمْ عَذَابًا أَلِيمًا وَيَسْتَبْدِلْ قَوْمًا غَيْرَكُمْ وَلاَ تَضُرُّوهُ شَيْئًا وَاللّهُ عَلَى كُلِّ شَيْءٍ
قَدِيرٌ﴿ ﴾التوبة/39 [134]

هَاأَنتُمْ هَؤُلاَء تُدْعَوْنَ لِتُنفِقُوا فِي سَبِيلِ اللّهِ فَمِنكُم مَّن يَبْخَلُ وَمَن يَبْخَلْ فَإِنَّمَا يَبْخَلُ عَن
نَّفْسِهِ وَاللّهُ الْغَنِيُّ وَأَنتُمُ الْفُقَرَاء وَإِن تَتَوَلَّوْا يَسْتَبْدِلْ قَوْمًا غَيْرَكُمْ ثُمَّ لَا يَكُونُوا أَمْثَالَكُمْ
﴿﴾محمد/38 [135]

One should focus the critical expression of the replacement of a group as mentioned in above ayahs as وَيَسْتَبْدِلْ قَوْمًا غَيْرَكُمْ.

One should remember that group identities can be killing and devastating. The only group identity that we have and always proud is being a Muslim.

Even this identity is very clearly elaborated in the Qurān that the identity of being a Muslim does not only belong to us with the religion of Islām with Rasulullah ﷺ but it was always there as an inclusive identity with other prophets and their followers such as Ibrahim as, Musa as, Yusuf as, Isa as and others. In this regard, being a Muslim is not classical tagged club identity, but it is the purpose of life and existence as mentioned by Yusuf as with the expression رَبِّ قَدْ آتَيْتَنِي مِنَ تَوَفَّنِي مُسْلِمًا in الْمُلْكِ وَعَلَّمْتَنِي مِن تَأْوِيلِ الأَحَادِيثِ فَاطِرَ السَّمَاوَاتِ وَالأَرْضِ أَنتَ وَلِيِّي فِي الدُّنُيَا وَالآخِرَةِ تَوَفَّنِي مُسْلِمًا وَأَلْحِقْنِي بِالصَّالِحِينَ ﴿﴾يوسف/101 [136].

In this regard, one really tragically smile and feel sad when the person constantly witness these killing group identities as a X group, Y group movement, Z mosque community and etc.

Naming something as a group and moving with people along to a goal on the path of Allah ﷻ is a virtue.

Yet, if this group is not constantly reminded to reset this identity to a zero level as a pseudo and fake hindering identity in the realities of a being a humble a'bd as a Muslim in front of Allah ﷻ, then this engagement can be test for the group, the individuals in the group and the group leads. May Allah ﷻ protect us, Amìn.

---

134. If you do not go forth, He will punish you with a painful punishment and will replace you with another people, and you will not harm Him at all. And Allah is over all things competent.
135. Here you are - those invited to spend in the cause of Allah - but among you are those who withhold [out of greed]. And whoever withholds only withholds [benefit] from himself; and Allah is the Free of need, while you are the needy. And if you turn away, He will replace you with another people; then they will not be the likes of you.
136. My Lord, You have given me [something] of sovereignty and taught me of the interpretation of dreams. Creator of the heavens and earth, You are my protector in this world and in the Hereafter. Cause me to die a Muslim and join me with the righteous."

One of the signs of a healthy group movement is support all the virtuous actions outside the group, encourage them and be involved in their formation. If the group has an approach such that "if our group did not start this initiative or if our does not fully own this action, then we are not involved", then these are signs of a diseased group engagement, which can attract the displeasure of Allah ﷻ with trials and tests leading to earthquakes shaking the group and group movement with a possible destruction. May Allah ﷻ protect us, Amìn.

Sometimes, Allah ﷻ can give openings to a group and uphold them in integrity due to their certain practice that Allah ﷻ can be pleased much.

This can be the group's engagement in the love of Rasulullah ﷺ and its teachings and reminders around it. Due this engagement, Allah ﷻ can open the doors of a lot of khayr.

Another can be the group's enagement in one of the practices of Rasulullah ﷺ such as making good mashawarah-istisharah in decision making not promoting superiority of the self, or a charismatic leader. This indicate being a true a'bd in front of Allah ﷻ. Due this engagement, Allah ﷻ can open the doors of a lot of khayr.

There can be other specific virtues of a group that can uphold the continuity of the group. The pleasure of Allah ﷻ always embedded in practices of Rasulullah ﷺ.

Yet, when the group identities become much more pronounced beyond being a simple a'bd of Allah ﷻ with humbleness and humility in front of Allah ﷻ as a Muslim, then May Allah ﷻ protect us, there can be trials or tests, Allahu A'lam.

One should remember that when a person is in their death bed, the only meaningful group identity is being a Muslim as pillar at its essential and foundational level. Yet, being in a group and working together is very critical and important. Yet, in our self-accountability of resetting ourselves daily and constantly, our real identity forms when we are Muslim in front of Allah ﷻ as an individual as an a'bd. Therefore, implying our arrogance of self-ego-nafs, embedded in group identities of matter such as being a fire vs mud, color being white vs black, ethnicity being Arab vs non-Arab, country being American vs non-American, all with others can be deadly on the true path of Allah ﷻ.

Astagfirullah!

May Allah ﷻ protect us from our own selves, Amìn

May Allah 🌸 make us follow the path of Rasulullah 🌺, Amìn
Allahumma Salli Ala Sayyidina wa Habìbina Muhammad, 🌺.

Juz 27

Sûrah 51 al-Thãriyãt

[50][137]

Running to Allah 🌸 or not

فَفِرُّوا إِلَى اللهِ إِنِّي لَكُم مِّنْهُ نَذِيرٌ مُّبِينٌ

{الذاريات/50}

One should know that Allah 🌸 is al-Hayy and al-Qayyum. When we feel
again and again stressed and depressed, we need to run back to Allah 🌸
without any means.

The name of running back to Allah 🌸 can be by talking with Allah
🌸 referred as dua.

The name of running back to Allah can be by reminding the
self about the teachings from Allah 🌸 referred as the recitation and
implementation of the Qurãn and Hadith-Sunnah.

The name of running back to Allah 🌸 can be by thinking about
the creation and ni'mahs of Allah 🌸 referred as making tafakkur and
tadabbur.

All are different forms of running back to Allah 🌸.

They can be implemented together or separately.

One should remember that in a day, we are constantly at the verge of
decision making either running back to Allah 🌸 or not.

In the case of running back to Allah 🌸, one should remember
that hope, purpose, meaning and activeness are all real and upholding
perspectives of structure and imãn.

Yet in the absence of running back to Allah 🌸, hopelessness,
purposelessness, laziness, and heedlessness are all false and destructive
perspectives of chaos, and kufr.

---

137. So flee to Allah. Indeed, I am to you from Him a clear warner.

Therefore, if a person deems a pessimistic life perspective especially fueled with kufr indicating the absence of running back to Allah ﷻ, in reality, accuses all the creation without any purpose and meaning and assumes the absence of Allah ﷻ, Astagfirullah!

Therefore, the person of kufr deems accountability and recompense for his or her false accusation and slander for all the creation and the Creator, Astagfirullah!

May Allah ﷻ protect us from the darkness of kufr even less than a second, Amìn!

May Allah ﷻ do not leave us with our own selves even less than a second, Amìn!

Allahumma Salli ala Sayyidina wa Habibinā Muhammad ﷺ.

[56]¹³⁸

وَمَا خَلَقْتُ الْجِنَّ وَالْإِنسَ إِلَّا لِيَعْبُدُونِ

{الذاريات/56}

Tree of Diseases & its Treatment: Ownership of the Heart and Maintenance of the Mind

One should remember that our hearts need constant purification.

One of the main purposes of our existence is the purification of hearts from the real diseases.

The real diseases are the diseases that affect one's life in this world and after one die.

Jealousy is a disease that destroys the person by constant questioning the decree and will of Allah ﷻ, Astagfirullah! The opposite of hasad-jealousy is to submit oneself to the decree of Allah ﷻ with taslìm, tawakkul, and ta'wiz.

Showing off is a disease that the person constantly seeks human existence and awareness in one's actions, Astagfirullah!

Yet, if the person does something by focusing only on La ilaha illa Allah, then this is the purity, healthiness, and safety. The opposite of showing off is sincerity-ikhlas. Doing things and seeking awareness,

---

138. And I did not create the jinn and mankind except to worship Me.

acceptance and pleasure only for and from Allah ﷻ in all the engagements is the definition of ikhlās-sincerity.

It is encouraged to prefer solitude in mountains in self-reflection/ accountability-tafakkur as a venue, and seclusion in time by getting up in the middle of the night and praying such as tahajjud. Although there can be riya-show off in these cases, yet one tries to minimize these effects by removing the causalities serving as blocks and veils in order to help the person focus on oneself with his or relation with Allah ﷻ with La ilaha illa Allah.

Arrogance is a disease that the person constantly judges others and ultimately dares to Decree and Will of Allah ﷻ. Everything for this person implies the superiority and deity of his or her ego, Astagfirullah! The opposite of arrogance-kibr is faqr-ajz of being as a real a'bd-ubudiyyah in front of Allah ﷻ with true humility and humbleness.

Therefore, among all the diseases, the most dangerous is considered as kibr-arrogance because the person opposes to be the a'bd of Allah ﷻ. This is opposite of the reality of[139] {الذاريات/65} وَمَا خَلَقْتُ الْجِنَّ وَالْإِنْسَ إِلَّا لِيَعْبُدُونِ

Arrogance leads to kufr, explicitly leading to claim a deity other than Allah ﷻ. Arrogance is the opposite of La ilaha illa Allah.

Therefore, the person who has the tiny size of this disease of arrogance-kibr in their heart and dying in this state can put the person in Jahannam even though he or she says that he or she is a Muslim. This is mentioned in the hadith [11]. May Allah ﷻ protect us, Amìn.

The second is the branch or branching of the primary disease of arrogance. This is riyā-showing off. Although the person may not have arrogance-kibr, yet not focusing on Allah ﷻ as the Only, and One Creator, the person seeks benefits from others as the implied deities. When we review the history of early Meccans, they accepted Allah ﷻ but they had also other deities that they used to explicitly seek benefit from them.

This is called in terminology as shirk. When it is done explicitly, it is referred as explicit Shirk. Explicit shirk can lead to kufr. If it is done implicitly, then it is called implicit shirk. Implicit shirk can also lead to hypocrisy, a person who really hides their real identity. The hycpocrites are at the lowest part of Jahannam, May Allah ﷻ protect us, Amìn. For Muslims, implicit shirk can lead to fisq, a person with sins.

---

139. And I did not create the jinn and mankind except to worship Me.

This is unfortunately can be common among believers-Muslims as Rasulullah ﷺ mentioned that he ﷺ was worried about this disease of shirk among the ummah as it was similar to a dark ant walking in a dark room [10] as mentioned in the hadith. Another hadith about the first three people to be thrown in the Jahannam, May Allah ﷻ protect us, to be the people externally being a Muslim but sought other means in their engagement of religious matters other than Allah ﷻ again referred as riya-showing off [9]. Riya leads to shirk. Shirk is the branch of kufr.

Lastly, one can consider and view jealousy as the fruit of the tree with the roots of arrogance representing kufr, branches of showing off-riya representing shirk, and fruits of jealousy representing not being a real Muslim. Yes, the disease of jealousy fumes the fire of not being pleased about the decree of Allah ﷻ on others. This shows a rejection on the part of the person to submit to the Will of Allah ﷻ. Whoever rejects to submit to the Will of Allah ﷻ is not a true Muslim. Being a Muslim requires a full submission to the Will of Allah ﷻ about What Allah ﷻ decreed on the person. For example, if a person has a problem about the selection of a prophet or the Prophet ﷺ, then this is jealousy. Historically, the people who had the problem with the selection of Allah ﷻ with the prophets did not become Muslim.

One can depict these three spiritual diseases as:

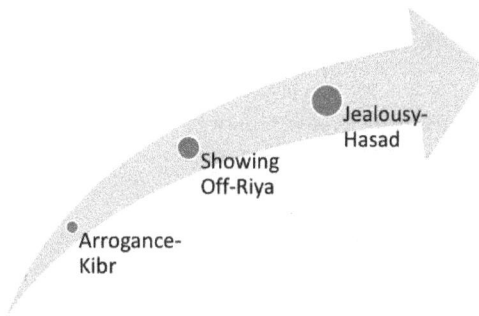

Jealousy-Hasad

Showing Off-Riya

Arrogance-Kibr

As kibr-arrogance can be the root disease, riya-showing-off can be trunk of this tree and jealousy-hasad can be the fruits of it. In this sense jealousy is the most visible, relevant and noticable part of this sequence in human interactions. Kibr-arrogance can be the root disease feeding other diseases but it can be less visible but only true known by Allah ﷻ. May Allah ﷻ protect us. On the other hand, showing-off/riya can be sometimes visible and sometimes not, depending on the case and type.

Yes, the real purpose of our existence is really to detect those diseases in our hearts and mind. Heart feels it and holds it and mind rationalizes it and maintains it.

For these diseases, ownership of the heart induces the feelings of worry, depression and stress and maintenance of the mind forms doubts, insecurity and instability, SubhanAllah!

In treatment of these diseases, one can start with the mind to break the maintenance by showing that arrogance, showing off and jealousy really does not make sense. When there is not a good maintenance in a house, then that the house will not survive and eventually collapse.

Then, the owner who is the heart will lose the ownership or if he is smart enough, the heart will sell this ownership before it loses it.

On the other hand, one can also show the heart alternative ownerships such as the feelings through sakina, peace, tranquility, calmness gained by Dhikrullah compared to the feelings of anger, depression, and agitation induced by arrogance, showing off and jealousy. Dhikrullah is the best house of the heart. Heart holds it and owns it and mind maintains it.

Maintenance of the house comes with the constant making correct choice of engagements with the correct and efficient workers of Dhikrullah. In that sense, mind needs to use constantly the free-will choice of hiring the right people for Dhikrullah for maintenance. The best and efficient associates of Dhikrullah is the Qurān and Sunnah of Rasulullah ﷺ.

Yes, as one tastes different feelings with Dhikrullah, then heart can desire to own the real and profitable feelings of sakina directly connected to Allah ﷻ. Then, the heart looks at itself and says "how silly I was, I was connecting myself with ego-nafs as a fake deity and I was suffering, now alhamdulillah I found the guidance."

One can depict the dynamics of the heart and mind with responsibilities as:

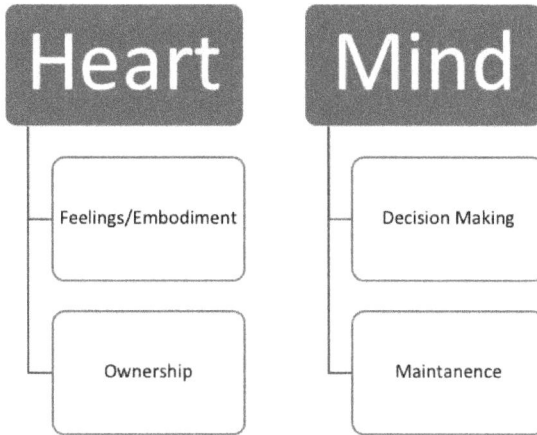

Heart

- Feelings/Embodiment
- Ownership

Mind

- Decision Making
- Maintanence

Yet, we carry the nafs-ego with us until we die. It will naturally constantly desire connecting the person with it. Therefore, there is a struggle. Mind needs to struggle for the right choice with the free-will and choice. Heart needs to feel and embody the humbleness and humility in front of Allah ﷻ for constantly asking the guidance for the right choice as mentioned[140] إِيَّاكَ نَعْبُدُ وإِيَّاكَ نَسْتَعِينُ {الفاتحة/5} اهدِنَا الصِّرَاطَ المُسْتَقِيمَ {الفاتحة/6} صِرَاطَ الَّذِينَ أَنعَمتَ عَلَيهِمْ غَيرِ المَغضُوبِ عَلَيهِمْ وَلاَ الضَّالِّينَ {الفاتحة/7}

The environments and engagements of Dhikrullah needs the choice of the person with his or her free will.

Therefore, the gist and purpose of one's existence is to make the choice of being in the state of Dhikrullah and with the people of Dhikrullah. That is the secrecy of free-will.

All the engagements of Dhikrullah ﷻ is called ubudiyyah and ibadah of Allah ﷻ.

May Allah ﷻ make us do the right choice according to our purpose of creation, Amìn.

May Allah ﷻ clean our hearts and minds from all types of diseases, Amìn.

---

140. **[1:5]** It is You we worship and You we ask for help. **[1:6]** Guide us to the straight path -**[1:7]** The path of those upon whom You have bestowed favor, not of those who have evoked [Your] anger or of those who are astray.

أَللّهُمَّ صَلِّ على سَيِّدِنا مُحَمَّد وعلى آل سيدنا محمد كَمَا صَلَّيْتَ على سَيِّدِنا إبراهيم وعلى آل سيدنا إبراهيم إنك حميد مجيد

Allahumma Salli ala Sayyidina Muhammad wa ala āli Sayyidina Muhammad ﷺ Kama Sallayta a'la Sayyidina Ibrahìm wa ala āli Sayyidina Ibrahim Innaka Hamìdun Majìd.

Juz 28

Sûrah 64 al-Taghābun

[14-18][141]

Detachment from Everything and Attachment to Only Allah ﷻ

يَا أَيُّهَا الَّذِينَ آمَنُوا إِنَّ مِنْ أَزْوَاجِكُمْ وَأَوْلَادِكُمْ عَدُوًّا لَكُمْ فَاحْذَرُوهُمْ وَإِن تَعْفُوا وَتَصْفَحُوا وَتَغْفِرُوا فَإِنَّ اللَّهَ غَفُورٌ رَحِيمٌ {التغابن/14} إِنَّمَا أَمْوَالُكُمْ وَأَوْلَادُكُمْ فِتْنَةٌ وَاللَّهُ عِندَهُ أَجْرٌ عَظِيمٌ {التغابن/15} فَاتَّقُوا اللَّهَ مَا اسْتَطَعْتُمْ وَاسْمَعُوا وَأَطِيعُوا وَأَنفِقُوا خَيْرًا لِأَنفُسِكُمْ وَمَن يُوقَ شُحَّ نَفْسِهِ فَأُولَٰئِكَ هُمُ الْمُفْلِحُونَ {التغابن/16} إِن تُقْرِضُوا اللَّهَ قَرْضًا حَسَنًا يُضَاعِفْهُ لَكُمْ وَيَغْفِرْ لَكُمْ وَاللَّهُ شَكُورٌ حَلِيمٌ {التغابن/17} عَالِمُ الْغَيْبِ وَالشَّهَادَةِ الْعَزِيزُ الْحَكِيمُ {التغابن/18}

One should remember that the person should not attach oneself to anything or anyone except Allah ﷻ. This can be indicated as يَا أَيُّهَا الَّذِينَ آمَنُوا إِنَّ مِنْ أَزْوَاجِكُمْ وَأَوْلَادِكُمْ عَدُوًّا لَكُمْ فَاحْذَرُوهُمْ

Anything or anyone around the person can be a test and trial for the person.

One should not attach one's heart to anyone or anything except Allah ﷻ.

A person should love something or someone for the sake of Allah ﷻ.

This means the bonding relationship of love or attachment comes due to the love of Allah ﷻ but not for the essence of that thing or a person.

---

141. **[64:14]** O you who have believed, indeed, among your wives and your children are enemies to you, so beware of them. But if you pardon and overlook and forgive - then indeed, Allah is Forgiving and Merciful. **[64:15]** Your wealth and your children are but a trial, and Allah has with Him a great reward. **[64:16]** So fear Allah as much as you are able and listen and obey and spend [in the way of Allah]; it is better for yourselves. And whoever is protected from the stinginess of his soul - it is those who will be the successful. **[64:17]** If you loan Allah a goodly loan, He will multiply it for you and forgive you. And Allah is Most Appreciative and Forbearing. **[64:18]** Knower of the unseen and the witnessed, the Exalted in Might, the Wise.

Therefore, a person of Allah ﷻ who has this bonding relationship with him or herself can implement the teachings of وَإِن تَعْفُوا وَتَصْفَحُوا وَتَغْفِرُو when they face the challenges, trials and tests with this attached item or thing.

If the person loves something or someone for or with their essence due to the veiling or blockage in one's nafs as mentioned شُحَّ نَفْسِهِ but not through the bond of relation with Allah ﷻ, then the person cannot implement وَإِن تَعْفُوا وَتَصْفَحُوا وَتَغْفِرُو. Yet, the person can loose and become very frustrated, agitated and angry when that thing or loved one detach themselves from the person.

The bonding to everything and everyone through the preferences and love of Allah ﷻ is the safest, most authentic and rewarding approach for the person.

When the thing or that person shows the human side of unappreciative attitude, then the lover normalizes this attitude and says "I was expecting this and it happened, the Only One Who does not turn away from the person is Allah ﷻ. " Allah ﷻ is al-Shakûr, All-Appreciative. Allah ﷻ is al-Hayy and al-Qayyum All-Living and All-Continuous.

One can realize this reality as[142] إِن تُقْرِضُوا اللَّهَ قَرْضًا حَسَنًا يُضَاعِفْهُ لَكُمْ وَيَغْفِرْ لَكُمْ وَاللَّهُ شَكُورٌ حَلِيمٌ {التغابن/17} عَالِمُ الْغَيْبِ وَالشَّهَادَةِ الْعَزِيزُ الْحَكِيمُ {التغابن/18}

Yes, our frustrations in life can be less painful and be normalized when we truly turn our hearts, and expectations only to Allah ﷻ.

Yes, our frustrations in life can be less painful and be normalized when we know and expect any time a possible detachment from a loved one except Allah ﷻ.

Yes, our frustrations in life can be less painful and be normalized when we only love and establish relationships with people through the rope of love and preferences of Allah ﷻ indicated by this love.

Loving Allah ﷻ requires the preferences as indicated in the Qurān and sunnah of Rasulullah ﷺ.

It is not mere love that the person says "I love You Ya Allah!, I love You Ya Rasulullah ﷺ!" and really if this does not care much about the preferences as instructed in the Qurān and Sunnah of Rasulullah ﷺ.

---

142. **[64:17]**If you loan Allah a goodly loan, He will multiply it for you and forgive you. And Allah is Most Appreciative and Forbearing. **[64:18]** Knower of the unseen and the witnessed, the Exalted in Might, the Wise.

If the person is a sinner and cannot implement these preferences fully in his or her life, at least he or she should feel the pain of regret, shame and embarrassment in front of Allah ﷻ as "Ya Allah ﷻ I love You yet, I can't fulfil my promises, every day, I am in ups and downs, please forgive my short comings." The expression فَٱتَّقُوا اللَّهَ مَا ٱسْتَطَعْتُمْ can indicate this reality.

In reality, if one analyzes the content of the sayyidul istighfār as mentioned by Rasulullah salallahu alayhi wa sallam [12], the expression of فَٱتَّقُوا اللَّهَ مَا ٱسْتَطَعْتُمْ mentioned in this istighfār as well. The sultan or king of all istighfār referred as the sayyidul istighfār is an inner disposition of the person that one should embody regardless of being sinner or not in the relationship of the person with Allah ﷻ.

اللهُم جعلنا منهم، آمين

Allahumma Ja'alna minhum, Amìn.

اللهُمَّ صَلِّ عَلَى سَيِّدِنَا وَ حَبِيبِنَا مُحَمَّد ﷺ

Allahumma Salli Sayyidina wa Habìbina Muhammad ﷺ.

Sûrah 66

Our Pains of Being in Different Roles in Life & the Institution of Family

يَا أَيُّهَا الَّذِينَ آمَنُوا قُوا أَنفُسَكُمْ وَأَهْلِيكُمْ نَارًا وَقُودُهَا النَّاسُ وَالْحِجَارَةُ عَلَيْهَا مَلَائِكَةٌ غِلَاظٌ شِدَادٌ لَا يَعْصُونَ اللَّهَ مَا أَمَرَهُمْ وَيَفْعَلُونَ مَا يُؤْمَرُونَ {التحريم/6}[143]

One should remember that Allah ﷻ sees the person and knows all the inside and outside conditions of the person. Allah ﷻ is al-Zāhir, al-Batin and as mentioned[144] وَلَقَدْ خَلَقْنَا الْإِنسَانَ وَنَعْلَمُ مَا تُوَسْوِسُ بِهِ نَفْسُهُ وَنَحْنُ أَقْرَبُ إِلَيْهِ مِنْ حَبْلِ الْوَرِيدِ {ق/16}

Sometimes, the frustrations from our own selves and others can put us in the states of different external and internal turmoil.

In these states of chaos, the person should try to stick to the engagements of mind in order to minimize the aftermath damages of these spiritual storms similar to lake effect snow. These states can be

---

143. O you who have believed, protect yourselves and your families from a Fire whose fuel is people and stones, over which are [appointed] angels, harsh and severe; they do not disobey Allah in what He commands them but do what they are commanded.

144. And We have already created man and know what his soul whispers to him, and We are closer to him than [his] jugular vein

similar to a person sailing in the ocean with a weak boat and about to sink as mentioned[145] وَإِذَا غَشِيَهُم مَّوْجٌ كَالظُّلَلِ دَعَوُا اللَّهَ مُخْلِصِينَ لَهُ الدِّينَ فَلَمَّا نَجَّاهُمْ إِلَى الْبَرِّ فَمِنْهُم مُّقْتَصِدٌ وَمَا يَجْحَدُ بِآيَاتِنَا إِلَّا كُلُّ خَتَّارٍ كَفُورٍ {لقمان/32}

Yes, our boats are very weak. We can sink at any time if there is no help, support and life vest from Allah ﷻ.

The bumpy and wavy journeys of life induce much pain and form sometimes the states of frozen spiritual faculties.

As the person is at the highest level of weakness with these changing and gushing feelings of self-blame, guilt, hating oneself and hating others, there is always a life vest from Allah ﷻ if he or she has a little bit inclination or push oneself with dua to Allah ﷻ.

Yes, we have different roles in life. A role as a parent, a role as a child, a role as a friend, a role as sister or brother, a role as a coworker, husband or wife, and many others. Each role we are in can seem to be changing. Yet, there is one essential and primary role that establishes and shapes other roles.

That is, our primary relationship with Allah ﷻ shaping and forming our intention in our all engagements of life.

Sometimes, humans self-interested based motivations can shape the roles. Yet, this can be at all times painful without any exception.

Let's assume a case of a couple married for twenty years. Even in a perfect-seeming marriage, there will be, for sure, some frustrations sometimes in this relationship. In this relationship, if the person bases this covenant only on self-interests but not viewing marriage as an institution that its benefits emerge for others such as children, bond ships, families, social and other engagements, then this institution will fail. With a similar approach, there will not be any corporations, or organizations promoting good in large as a group movement.

One should remember that group movements for ethical actions do not start in the church, mosque, synagogue, or temples but it starts at home in the institution of families.

---

145. And when waves come over them like canopies, they supplicate Allah, sincere to Him in religion [i.e., faith]. But when He delivers them to the land, there are [some] of them who are moderate [in faith]. And none rejects Our signs except everyone treacherous and ungrateful.

The focus in the institution of family is critical as mentioned in the ayah as[146] يَا أَيُّهَا الَّذِينَ آمَنُوا قُوا أَنفُسَكُمْ وَأَهْلِيكُمْ نَارًا وَقُودُهَا النَّاسُ وَالْحِجَارَةُ عَلَيْهَا مَلَائِكَةٌ غِلَاظٌ شِدَادٌ لَا يَعْصُونَ اللَّهَ مَا أَمَرَهُمْ وَيَفْعَلُونَ مَا يُؤْمَرُونَ {التحريم/6}

Islām started as a group movement in the family of Rasulullah ﷺ with Khadija (رضي الله عنها), Ali (رضي الله عنه), and Zayd (رضي الله عنه) extending to others. We remember this group movement in our salawat to implement in our lives as Allahumma Salli ala a'li Sayyidina Muhammad.

Judaism started as a group movement in the family of Ibrahim as with Hājar (رضي الله عنها), Ismael (عليه السلام), Sarah (رضي الله عنها), Ishāq (عليه السلام) extending to Yāqûb (عليه السلام) with his 12 children including Yusuf (عليه السلام). We remember this group movement in our salawat to implement in our lives as Allahumma Salli ala a'li Sayyidina Ibrāhìm.

Christianity started as a group movement in the family of Imrān with Zakariyya (عليه السلام), Yahya-John the Baptist (عليه السلام), and Maryam (عليه السلام) giving birth to Isa (عليه السلام). We remember this group movement in our teaching that Jesus will come in his second coming before the End of Days bringing once more peace on the earth.

One should remember that the Qurān mentions and spends extensive portions on the above families and indicates the importance of group movements starting in the families for a change in society at large.

Unfortunately, today since we forget our primary and essential role with Allah ﷻ shaping other roles, then every other role becomes very blurry. The relationships at different parts of our lives always then induce pain, making us miserable due to not having a primary purpose or intention of why we are in these relationships.

May Allah ﷻ forgive us, and guide us, Amìn.

May Allah ﷻ do not leave us with our own selves alone even less than a second, Amìn.

May Allah ﷻ clean and purify our intentions to the direction that Allah ﷻ is pleased, Amìn.

اللهُمَّ صَلِّ عَلَى سَيِّدِنَا وَ حَبِيْبِنَا مُحَمَّد ﷺ المصطفى

Allahumma Salli a'lā Sayyidina wa Habìbina Muhammad ﷺ al-Mustafa ﷺ.

---

146. O you who have believed, protect yourselves and your families from a Fire whose fuel is people and stones, over which are [appointed] angels, harsh and severe; they do not disobey Allah in what He commands them but do what they are commanded.

Juz 29

Sûrah 70 al-Ma'ârij

[4][147]

Relativity of Time: Removing the Boundaries of Time & Infinite Life in the Afterlife

تَعْرُجُ الْمَلَائِكَةُ وَالرُّوحُ إِلَيْهِ فِي يَوْمٍ كَانَ مِقْدَارُهُ خَمْسِينَ أَلْفَ سَنَةٍ
{المعارج/4}

One should remember that as humans we are bound in time in this life.

Although there are the clock counters measuring the time, this time can be expanded and constricted. One can call this relativity of time in classical Einsteinian physics. In the worlds of reality, for the people of heart, ahlullah, a similar notion is expressed with the terms of bast and qabz, expansion and contraction of time.

One should first define the terms and principles of this reality of time before the worlds of experience as in the incase of ahlullah or before detailed dealings of the people of natural sciences dealing with physics or laws as established by Allah ﷻ.

The first and major principle is that one can actually transform one second or less than a second into years as also mentioned[148] لَيْلَةُ الْقَدْرِ خَيْرٌ مِّنْ أَلْفِ شَهْرٍ {القدر/3}.

How do we do this transform? It is very simple and real.

This is when a person spends a second with ikhlâs-sincerity on the path of Allah ﷻ Who is al-Bakî, the Infinite, then this person's one second engagement is transformed into years, thousand years, or beyond the time. The ayah[149] تَعْرُجُ الْمَلَائِكَةُ وَالرُّوحُ إِلَيْهِ فِي يَوْمٍ كَانَ مِقْدَارُهُ خَمْسِينَ أَلْفَ سَنَةٍ {المعارج/4} can allude some of the glimpses from this reality.

Because, the struggle is on the path of the One Who is not bind to time, space or anything but everything is bind under the One, Allah ﷻ.

---

147. The angels and the Spirit will ascend to Him during a Day the extent of which is fifty thousand years.

148. The Night of Decree is better than a thousand months.

149. The angels and the Spirit will ascend to Him during a Day the extent of which is fifty thousand years.

In this regard, one can carefully analyze the ayah as[150] وَمَنْ أَرَادَ الْآخِرَةَ وَسَعَى لَهَا سَعْيَهَا وَهُوَ مُؤْمِنٌ فَأُولَئِكَ كَانَ سَعْيُهُم مَّشْكُورًا {الإسراء/19}

The effort of the person as mentioned with the word سَعَى is all recorded and placed in a category of transformation with results.

Everyone's effort is being accounted as mentioned[151] فَمَن يَعْمَلْ مِنَ الصَّالِحَاتِ وَهُوَ مُؤْمِنٌ فَلَا كُفْرَانَ لِسَعْيِهِ وَإِنَّا لَهُ كَاتِبُونَ {الأنبياء/94}

In this regard, although our efforts may seem a second or so, Allah ۞ gives its results fully beyond the time in the afterlife as mentioned[152]

أَلَّا تَزِرُ وَازِرَةٌ وِزْرَ أُخْرَى {النجم/38} وَأَن لَّيْسَ لِلْإِنسَانِ إِلَّا مَا سَعَى {النجم/39} وَأَنَّ سَعْيَهُ سَوْفَ يُرَى {النجم/40} ثُمَّ يُجْزَاهُ الْجَزَاءَ الْأَوْفَى {النجم/41} وَأَنَّ إِلَى رَبِّكَ الْمُنتَهَى {النجم/42} وَأَنَّهُ هُوَ أَضْحَكَ وَأَبْكَى {النجم/43} وَأَنَّهُ هُوَ أَمَاتَ وَأَحْيَا {النجم/44}

All of our engagements or efforts regardless on the path of Allah ۞ or not, with ikhlās or without are all different as mentioned[153] إِنَّ سَعْيَكُمْ لَشَتَّى {الليل/4}

In this sense, if one wants to expand their time, outcomes and results, he or she should put all their effort on path of the One Who is al-Bāki. Then, his or her efforts can have barakah and ease with the transformation of the outputs beyond time as mentioned[154] فَأَمَّا مَن أَعْطَى وَاتَّقَى {الليل/5} وَصَدَّقَ بِالْحُسْنَى {الليل/6} فَسَنُيَسِّرُهُ لِلْيُسْرَى {الليل/7}

On the other hand, if a person spends all this life in their engagements without the One, Allah ۞, although he or she may seem to have a long fun life, in reality, there will be contraction in his or her time without

---

150. But whoever desires the Hereafter and exerts the effort due to it while he is a believer - it is those whose effort is ever appreciated [by Allah].
151. So whoever does righteous deeds while he is a believer - no denial will there be for his effort, and indeed We, of it, are recorders.
152. **[53:38]** That no bearer of burdens will bear the burden of another **[53:39]** And that there is not for man except that [good] for which he strives**[53:40]** And that his effort is going to be seen -**[53:41]** Then he will be recompensed for it with the fullest recompense**[53:42]** And that to your Lord is the finality **[53:43]** And that it is He who makes [one] laugh and weep**[53:44]**And that it is He who causes death and gives life
153. And [by] the night when it covers it
154. **[91:5]** And [by] the sky and He who constructed it **[91:6]** And [by] the earth and He who spread it **[91:7]** And [by] the soul and He who proportioned it

any barakah but difficulty as mentioned[155] {8/الليل} وَأَمَّا مَن بَخِلَ وَاسْتَغْنَى
وَكَذَّبَ بِالْحُسْنَى {9/الليل} فَسَنُيَسِّرُهُ لِلْعُسْرَى {10/الليل}

وَيَوْمَ تَقُومُ السَّاعَةُ يُقْسِمُ الْمُجْرِمُونَ مَا لَبِثُوا غَيْرَ سَاعَةٍ كَذَلِكَ كَانُوا
يُؤْفَكُونَ {55/الروم}[156] وَقَالَ الَّذِينَ أُوتُوا الْعِلْمَ وَالْإِيمَانَ لَقَدْ لَبِثْتُمْ
فِي كِتَابِ اللَّهِ إِلَى يَوْمِ الْبَعْثِ فَهَذَا يَوْمُ الْبَعْثِ وَلَكِنَّكُمْ كُنتُمْ لَا تَعْلَمُونَ
{56/الروم}[157]

SubhanAllah!

May Allah ﷻ accept our efforts and make all our seconds and
purpose of life to please Allah ﷻ on the path of Rasulullah ﷺ with ikhlās
and ihsān, Amìn.

اللهُمَّ صَلِّ عَلَى سَيِّدِنَا وَ حَبِيْبِنَا مُحَمّد ﷺ

Allahumma Salli A'la Sayyidina wa Habìbina Muhammad ﷺ.

Sûrah 75 al-Qiyãmah

[2]

وَلَا أُقْسِمُ بِالنَّفْسِ اللَّوَّامَةِ

{2/القيامة}[158]

يَا أَيَّتُهَا النَّفْسُ الْمُطْمَئِنَّةُ {27/الفجر}[159] ارْجِعِي إِلَى رَبِّكِ رَاضِيَةً مَّرْضِيَّةً {28/الفجر}[160]
فَادْخُلِي فِي عِبَادِي {29/الفجر}[161] وَادْخُلِي جَنَّتِي[162] {30/الفجر}

---

155. **[91:8]** And inspired it [with discernment of] its wickedness and its righteousness
[91:9] He has succeeded who purifies it **[91:10]** And he has failed who instills it [with
corruption].
156. And the Day the Hour appears the criminals will swear they had remained but an hour.
Thus, they were deluded.
157. But those who were given knowledge and faith will say, "You remained the extent of
Allah's decree until the Day of Resurrection, and this is the Day of Resurrection, but you did
not used to know."
158. And I swear by the reproaching soul [to the certainty of resurrection].
159. To the righteous it will be said, "O reassured soul,
160. Return to your Lord, well-pleased and pleasing [to Him],
161. And enter among My [righteous] servants
162. And enter My Paradise."

One should remember that Allah ﷻ is not pleased with any of our languages, and implications that may imply humiliation of others. Even, for some people, if this is at a thought or idea level, a real person of imān should be really disgusted about him or herself with the possibility of displeasing Allah ﷻ.

It is expected that a person of nafs-lawwamah does much lawm of his or her nafs and hopefully learns from his or her mistakes but moves the upper level of nafs-mutmainna.

Some of the people of nafs-lawwamah can be the ones who can be much action based on the path of Allah ﷻ. Therefore, in their self-accountability or self-muhasaba, after this action is over, then they may constantly engage themselves with lawm for the possibilities of displeasing Allah ﷻ.

For the elects of nafs-mutmainna or qalbun-salìm, they try to minimize the hit & miss type action engagements. They generally work around constantly hitting the target and winning on the path of Allah ﷻ without much displeasing Allah but always pleasing Allah ﷻ.

This state of nafs or Qalb require one of the highest forms of sabr-patience. Their talks are minimal. They are mostly in constant muraqaba and states of ihsān with tawakkaul, taslìm and ta'fiz. When they talk, they talk a few words but with hikmah from the heart breaking the darkness and pleasing Allah ﷻ.

The prime embodiment of this level and beyond is Rasulullah ﷺ. When one can review the life instances of Rasulullah ﷺ, the title of "Jawamul Kalim" is given to express exactly the few words of Rasulullah ﷺ with hikmah breaking the darkness and pleasing Allah ﷻ.

Rasulullah ﷺ was mostly in the state of silence with muraqaba, ihsān and wisdom.

The staging of nafs ammarah to nafs lawwamah, and then, nafs mutmainna or nafs radiyyah indicating Qalbun Salìm with tawakkul, taw'fiz and taslìm can be in steps or levels.

Yet, for Rasulullah ﷺ, it was already there without going through these stages with the Fadl and Rahmah of Allah ﷻ.

His ﷺ immediate image Abu Bakir ra can have the similar bounty of this level without going through these steps due to being friend of Rasulullah ﷺ from the early times.

Yet, for the other sahabahs, and Muslims, this staging can be present at different lengths.

Yet, for sahabah, since they were with Rasulullah ﷺ, they experienced and were transformed to the states of nafs-mutmainna with the mai'yyah (companionship) of Rasulullah to the states of nafs-radiya as the Qurān mentions[163] لَقَدْ رَضِيَ اللَّهُ عَنِ الْمُؤْمِنِينَ إِذْ يُبَايِعُونَكَ تَحْتَ الشَّجَرَةِ فَعَلِمَ مَا فِي قُلُوبِهِمْ فَأَنْزَلَ السَّكِينَةَ عَلَيْهِمْ وَأَثَابَهُمْ فَتْحًا قَرِيبًا {الفتح/81}.

This staging is mentioned as[164] يَا أَيَّتُهَا النَّفْسُ الْمُطْمَئِنَّةُ {الفجر/27} ارْجِعِي إِلَى رَبِّكِ رَاضِيَةً مَّرْضِيَّةً {الفجر/28} فَادْخُلِي فِي عِبَادِي {الفجر/29} وَادْخُلِي جَنَّتِي {الفجر/30}

For the other Muslims, in later generations after Rasulullah ﷺ, depending on the level of their teachers/Shayks having the silsila-chain all the way to Rasulullah ﷺ, can give effects of this transformation to the states of nafs mutmainna.

One should really see examples and live with these examples of nafs-mutmainna/radiyyah for transformations for their levels of the nafs. The presence of Rasulullah ﷺ transformed all the sahabah. Their level cannot be reached by later generations due to the ma'iyyah of Rasullullah ﷺ.

Today, there are a lot of Muslims with nafs-ammarah. Good Muslims among them are at the level of nafs-lawwamah. These good Muslims with nafs-lawwamah at least regret about their engagements and turn to Allah ﷻ constantly.

Yet, today, the Muslims of nafs-mutmainna may not be many as we are far from Rasulullah ﷺ. As the hadith indicates that before the end of day, Muslims would be many, but will be like foam, like the foam on the river [25] (hadith # 4297) which can indicate the lack of quality in their levels of nafs.

May Allah ﷻ give us istiqamah and make us reach the levels of nafs-mutmainna-radiyyah with Qalbun Salìm, Amìn

اللهُمَّ صَلِّ عَلَى سَيِّدِنَا وَ حَبِيبِنَا مُحَمَّد ﷺ

Allahumma Salli A'la Sayyidina wa Habìbina Muhammad ﷺ.

---

163. Certainly was Allah pleased with the believers when they pledged allegiance to you, [O Muhammad], under the tree, and He knew what was in their hearts, so He sent down tranquillity upon them and rewarded them with an imminent conquest

164. **27.**[To the righteous it will be said], "O reassured soul, **28.** Return to your Lord, well-pleased and pleasing [to Him], **29.** And enter among My [righteous] servants. **30.** And enter My Paradise."

Juz 30

Sûrah 78 al-Nabã

[35]¹⁶⁵

لَّا يَسْمَعُونَ فِيهَا لَغْوًا وَلَا كِذَّابًا

{النبأ/35}

Realities of This Life and Afterlife

One should remember the descriptions related with afterlife and unseen realities are all approximations to our understanding of mind and emotions which are bound to causality and social constructs of the habitat, culture and time that we are living in.

In other words, Allah ﷻ can equip humans in barzakh, qabr, the Day of Judgment and afterlife with different tools of mind or receptive faculties that may not be exactly the same as in this life.

One can also understand that the struggle is to increase and continue on the path of marifatullah in the afterlife with the Grace and Fadl of Allah ﷻ. In this regard, without being responsible of the free will in akhirah-afterlife, one can inshAllah can continue on the path of Marifatullah by experiencing different n'imahs of Allah ﷻ including the physical and emotional other ni'mahs in Jannah and Ru'yatullah.

Imam Ghazali rh mentions that the capacity or quality of the a'qil-intellect that we have in this life will be different than the a'qil in afterlife, SubhanAllah! Haza min fadli Rabbi!

In this life, one should remember that we are constantly under the salvo of evil effects and influences. These influences affect us emotionally and mentally. Refreshing one's imãn with La ilaha illa Allah is always critical [26].

Sometimes, we don't, or we can't detect the source of the problems due to our inability to focus or due to being heedless. Yet, regardless of its source, if the person makes a habit of refreshing one's imãn with La ilaha illa Allah, then the problems leading to anxiety, stress, or depression can vanish and disappear inshAllah.

---

165. No ill speech will they hear therein or any falsehood -

Five times salah, different times of nawāfil, connecting oneself constantly to the recitation of the Qurān and hadith, and all types of Dhikrullah as the remembrance of Allah ﷻ lead the person to the refreshment of La ilaha illa Allah.

In the akhirah, since there are not external or internal evil effects as mentioned[166] {35/النبأ} لاَ يَسْمَعُونَ فِيهَا لَغْوًا وَلاَ كِذَّابًا, the person does not feel the pain of these effects causing stress, depression and anxiety.

One should remember that the evil environment, society, relationships and nowadays social media all induce problems, stress, depression and anxiety due to the abundance of لَغْوًا وَ كِذَّابًا. The absence of this brings sakina the real happiness.

Allahumma Adkhilna Jannata Ma'a al-abrar fi hazihi dunya and fil akhirah, Amìn.

Allahumma Salli ala Sayyidina wa Habibina Muhammad ﷺ.

Sûrah 89 al-Fajr

Relationships, Sakina-tranquility and Istiqamah-Balance

فَأَمَّا الْإِنسَانُ إِذَا مَا ابْتَلَاهُ رَبُّهُ فَأَكْرَمَهُ وَنَعَّمَهُ فَيَقُولُ رَبِّي أَكْرَمَنِ {15/الفجر} وَأَمَّا إِذَا مَا ابْتَلَاهُ فَقَدَرَ عَلَيْهِ رِزْقَهُ فَيَقُولُ رَبِّي أَهَانَنِ {16/الفجر}

One should remember that our relationships with Allah ﷻ brings sakina-tranquility to us. Imān-belief, Islām-following the guidelines, Taslim-submission and Tawakkul-reliance are all the sources of this sakina-tranquility at different levels if the person can implement.

True imān-belief leading to taslìm-submission and tawakkul-reliance can make the person live a life of Jannah-Heaven in this world before he or she dies.

Taslim-submission and tawakkul-reliance to Allah ﷻ requires embodying husn-zann-positive perspective and discovering a hikmah-wisdom in all incidents of life whether they are good or evil seeming, showering on us from Allah ﷻ.

---

166. No ill speech will they hear therein or any falsehood -

Yet sometimes, we rush to judge and disconnect ourselves from Allah ﷻ in our human fitrah-nature as mentioned[167] وَإِذَا أَنْعَمْنَا عَلَى الْإِنْسَانِ أَعْرَضَ وَنَأَى بِجَانِبِهِ وَإِذَا مَسَّهُ الشَّرُّ فَذُو دُعَاءٍ عَرِيضٍ {فصلت/51}

Or[168], إِنَّ رَبَّكَ لَبِالْمِرْصَادِ {الفجر/41}

فَأَمَّا الْإِنْسَانُ إِذَا مَا ابْتَلَاهُ رَبُّهُ فَأَكْرَمَهُ وَنَعَّمَهُ فَيَقُولُ رَبِّي أَكْرَمَنِ {الفجر/51} وَأَمَّا إِذَا مَا ابْتَلَاهُ فَقَدَرَ عَلَيْهِ رِزْقَهُ فَيَقُولُ رَبِّي أَهَانَنِ {الفجر/61} كَلَّا بَل لَّا تُكْرِمُونَ الْيَتِيمَ {الفجر/71} وَلَا تَحَاضُّونَ عَلَى طَعَامِ الْمِسْكِينِ {الفجر/81} وَتَأْكُلُونَ التُّرَاثَ أَكْلًا لَّمًّا {الفجر/91} وَتُحِبُّونَ الْمَالَ حُبًّا جَمًّا {الفجر/02} ك

Yet, a person of hikmah and wisdom always adapts patience-sabr controlling one's heart and mind in all evil and good seeming incidents.

One call this as neutral state of heart and mind without any judgment. Another can call this state as attachment free of the heart and mind referred as zuhd.

Yet, in all these cases, zuhd or judgment or attachment free call of heart and mind indicate spiritual alertness referred as tayaqquz.

The absence of tayaqquz-spiritual alertness can make any incident a source of shirk and attachment of the heart and mind.

When there is the absence of tayaqquz-spiritual alertness, and when the person feels secure, then different levels of makr-trials and tests can hit the person to teach and remind the opposite reality.

The opposite reality is the positive uncertainty indicated by the states of tayaqquz that the person maintains the relationship with Allah ﷻ between the lines of hope and fear.

In this regard, the states of the heart and mind in imān-belief, Islām-following the guidelines, taslīm-submission, tawakkul-reliance, zuhd-judgment/attachment free states with tayaqquz-spiritual alertness with positive uncertainty keeps the person in istiqamah-balance.

Istiqamah-balance deems constant showering of sakina-tranquility on the heart and mind of the person in one's relationship with Allah ﷻ.

---

167. And when We bestow favor upon man, he turns away and distances himself; but when evil touches him, then he is full of extensive supplication.

168. Indeed, your Lord is in observation. And as for man, when his Lord tries him and [thus] is generous to him and favors him, he says, "My Lord has honored me." But when He tries him and restricts his provision, he says, "My Lord has humiliated me." No! But you do not honor the orphan. And you do not encourage one another to feed the poor. And you consume inheritance, devouring [it] altogether. And you love wealth with immense love.

Allahumma Salli a'la Sayyidina wa Habibina Muhammad ﷺ wa a'la ali sayyidina Muhammad ﷺ kama sallayta al'a Sayyidina Ibrahim (as) wa Sayyidina Mûsa (as) Sayyidina I'sa (as).

Diseases, Symptoms and Diagnosis

الَّذِينَ آمَنُواْ وَتَطْمَئِنُّ قُلُوبُهُم بِذِكْرِ اللّهِ أَلاَ بِذِكْرِ اللّهِ تَطْمَئِنُّ الْقُلُوبُ
{الرعد/28}

One should remember that Allah ﷻ is the only One to go constantly and relentlessly to go back with dua, istighfār, I'āna, help and protection.

One should remember our hearts are in the state of crying even if we realize or not.

When the tears reflect on our eyes, these can be realization points of the times that our hearts are crying.

Each crying with a tear is the representation of the crying of the heart.

At all times, the crying of the heart constantly tells the person that the heart yearns and desires to run to Allah ﷻ and calmed down and pacified with the remembrance of Allah ﷻ.

The ayah indicates this reality as mentioned

The times of gaflah induced in us and constantly displayed as contraction of heart of stress, anxiety, fear, terror and panic. In all these times, our hearts cry and ask help and beg to run Allah ﷻ.

Yet, when the person makes the habit of adapting other things except Allah ﷻ, the heart deepens this state of anguish into the diseases with trauma.

In this case, arrogance is a representation of trauma of the heart. Jealousy is a representation of the trauma of the heart. Showing off-riyā is a representation of this trauma of the heart.

On the other hand, the display of trauma in outer sciences or externalities or diagnosis in legal terminologies can be shirk, kufr, and others.

If we take for example, analyze one trauma case of riyā-showing off with its process, below can be a possible representation.

In the above diagram, traumatic disease of the heart displays its symptoms as showing-off riya. Then, its diagnosis in legal and official term becomes shirk.

In all engagements, there is no legal system of judging the people. Everyone is expected to establish their own self judiciary systems of judgments and prosecutors. At the end of the day, when the person dies, the Ultimate Judge, Allah ﷻ will reveal the person's fair or unfair judgments in this self-judiciary systems of courts only and truly known by the person and Allah ﷻ.

Therefore, in Islām and all the books sent by Allah ﷻ in human common court systems everything is based on externalities of implementation of social justices. It is illegal in this law system as instructed by the scriptures (shariāh)to execute a person due to his or her intention, thought or emotions that were displayed as action.

On the other hand, the execution of the Judgment in front of Allah ﷻ in afterlife is primarily based on this self-judiciary system of judgment based on the person's real intention and thoughts known only by the person and Allah ﷻ.

May Allah ﷻ make us establish a fair and a self-court system that is pleased by Allah ﷻ following the path of Rasulullah ﷺ, Amìn.

أللهُمَّ صَلِّ على سَيِّدِنا مُحَمَّد و على آله سيدنا محمد كَمَا صَلَّيْتَ على سَيِّدِنا إبراهيم وعلى آل سيدنا إبراهيم إنك حميد مجيد

[169]Allahumma Salli A'la Sayyidina Muhammad wa a'la a'li Sayyidina Muhammad Kama Sallayta a'la Sayyidina Ibrāhim wa a'la Sayyidina Ibrāhim Innaka Hāmidun Majìd

[170]Wa taqabbal minna bi hurmati malāikāti ajmāin wa husūsan bi hurmāti sayyidina Jibril, Ruhul Qudus wa Mikāil, Amin.

Diseases, Symptoms and Diagnosis

الَّذِينَ آمَنُواْ وَتَطْمَئِنُّ قُلُوبُهُم بِذِكْرِ اللّهِ أَلاَ بِذِكْرِ اللّهِ تَطْمَئِنُّ الْقُلُوبُ {الرعد/28}[171]

---

169. Oh God send our blessings and salutations on our role models Muhammad ﷺ, Abraham (عليه السلام), Jesus (عليه السلام), Moses (عليه السلام).

170. Oh God accept from us for the noble positions of all angels, especially Gabriel, the Holy Spirit and Michael, Amen.

171. Those who have believed and whose hearts are assured by the remembrance of Allah. Unquestionably, by the remembrance of Allah hearts are assured."

One should remember that Allah ﷻ is the only One to go constantly and relentlessly to go back with dua, istighfār, I'āna, help and protection.

One should remember our hearts are in the state of crying even if we realize or not.

When the tears reflect on our eyes, these can be realization points of the times that our hearts are crying.

Each crying with a tear is the representation of the crying of the heart.

At all times, the crying of the heart constantly tells the person that the heart yearns and desires to run to Allah ﷻ and calmed down and pacified with the remembrance of Allah ﷻ.

The ayah indicates this reality as mentioned

The times of gaflah induced in us and constantly displayed as contraction of heart of stress, anxiety, fear, terror and panic. In all these times, our hearts cry and ask help and beg to run Allah ﷻ .

Yet, when the person makes the habit of adapting other things except Allah ﷻ, the heart deepens this state of anguish into the diseases with trauma.

In this case, arrogance is a representation of trauma of the heart. Jealousy is a representation of the trauma of the heart. Showing off-riyā is a representation of this trauma of the heart.

On the other hand, the display of trauma in outer sciences or externalities or diagnosis in legal terminologies can be shirk, kufr, and others.

If we take for example, analyze one trauma case of riyā-showing off with its process, below can be a possible representation.

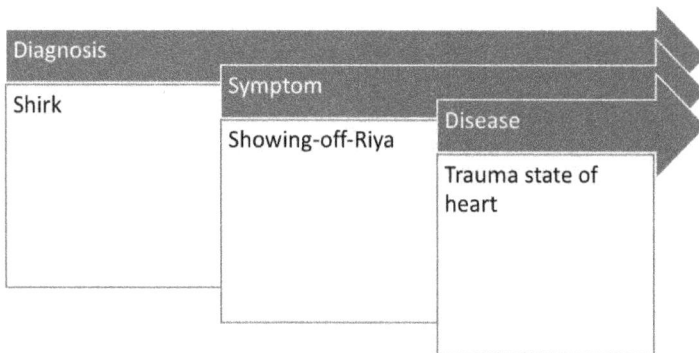

Diagnosis		
Shirk	Symptom	
	Showing-off-Riya	Disease
		Trauma state of heart

In the above diagram, traumatic disease of the heart displays its symptoms as showing-off riya. Then, its diagnosis in legal and official term becomes shirk.

In all engagements, there is no legal system of judging the people. Everyone is expected to establish their own self judiciary systems of judgments and prosecutors. At the end of the day, when the person dies, the Ultimate Judge, Allah ﷻ will reveal the person's fair or unfair judgments in this self-judiciary sytems of courts only and truly known by the person and Allah ﷻ.

Therefore, in Islām and all the books sent by Allah ﷻ in human commoncourt systems everything is based on externalities of implementation of social justices. It is illegal in this law system as instructed by the scriptures (shariāh)to execute a person due to his or her intention, thought or emotions that were displayed as action.

On the other hand, the execution of the Judgment in front of Allah ﷻ in afterlife is primarily based on this self-judiciary system of judgment based on the person's real intention and thoughts known only by the person and Allah ﷻ.

May Allah ﷻ make us establish a fair and a self-court system that is pleased by Allah ﷻ following the path of Rasulullah ﷺ, Amìn.

Allahumma Salli A'la Sayyidina Muhammad wa a'la a'li Sayyidina Muhammad Kama Sallayta a'la Sayyidina Ibrāhim wa a'la Sayyidina Ibrāhim Innaka Hāmidun Majìd

BIBLIOGRAPHY

[1] A. Muslim, Sahih Muslim (translated by Siddiqui, A.), Peace Vision, 1972.

[2] M. Razi, Mafatih al-Ghayb known as al-Tafsir al-Kabir, Cairo: Dar Ibya al-Kutub al-Bahiyya, 1172.

[3] U. P. Oxford, «Oxford Dictionaries,» 2016. [Online]. Available: http://www.oxforddictionaries.com/us/definition/american_english/. [Accessed 2016].

[4] I. A. `. M. at-Tirmidhī, Jami Tirmizi, Darus-Salam, 2017.

[5] S. Vahide, The Collection of Light, ihlas nur publication, 2001.

[6] M. Al-Bukhari, The translation of the meanings of Sahih Al-Bukhari, Kazi Publications, 1986.

[7] H. Baghawi, Tafsir al-Baghawi al-musamma Ma'alim al-tanzil, Bayrut: Dar al-Ma'rifah, 1987.

[8] M. b. '. al-Waqidi, The Life of Muhammad: Al-Waqidi›s Kitab Al-Maghazi, United Kingdom: Taylor & Francis., 2013, p. 26.

[9] Y. J. Kumek, Practical Mysticism: Sufi Journeys of Heart and Mind, Dubuque: Kendall Hunt, 2018.

[10] N. C. Ring, Introduction to the Study of Religion, New York: Orbis, 2007.

[11] A. I. Thalabi, Al-Kashaf wal bayan, Beirut: DKI, 2004.

[12] I. Malik, Al-Muwatta of Imam Malik Ibn Anas The First Formulation of Islamic Law (translator Aisha AbdurRahman Bewley), Kegan Paul International, 1989.

[13] S. T. B. A. j. A. Halveri, An excerpt from the most beautiful names, Threshold books, 1985.

[14] J. Suyuti, Tafsīr Al-Quran Al-Azīm (Commentary on the Quran), http://www.iqra.net/names/QuranNames.html ed., vol. 1, Darun Nadwa AlJadida, 1998, p. 50.

[15] SInternational, The Quran, Abul-Qasim Publishing House, 1997.

AUTHOR BIO

Dr. Kumek had classical training in Islamic sciences from the respected Shuyûqh/Teachers of Turkey, India, Egypt, Yemen, Somalia, Morocco, Sudan, and the United States. He stayed and studied classical Islamic sciences in Egypt and Turkey as well.

In his Western training, education and teaching experience, Dr. Kumek has acted as the religious studies coordinator at State University of New York (SUNY) Buffalo State and taught undergraduate and graduate courses in religious studies at SUNY at Buffalo State, Niagara University, Daemen College and Harvard Divinity School. Dr. Kumek also pursued doctorate degree in physics at SUNY at Buffalo published academic papers in the areas of quantum physics and medical physics. Then, he decided to engage with the world of social sciences through social anthropology, education, and cultural anthropology in his doctorate studies and subsequently, spent a few years as a research associate in the anthropology department of the same university and subsequently, completed a postdoctoral fellowship at Harvard Divinity school. Some of his book titles include sociology through religion, religious literacy through ethnography, selected passages from the Qurãn, selected passages from the Hadith (titled as Rasulullah ﷺ) and selected prayers of the Prophet Muhammad ﷺ (titled as Pearls and Diamonds). Dr. M. Yunus Kumek is currently teaching on Muslim Ministry and Spiritual Care at Harvard Divinity School.

ACKNOWLEDGMENTS

I would like to thank all my unnamed teachers, friends, and students for their input, ideas, suggestions, help, and support during and before the preparation of this book.

I would like to thank Dr. David Banks, faculty of the Department of Anthropology, State University of New York (SUNY), Sister Toni Hajdaj, Sister Umm Aisha, Dr. AbdulAhad, Br. Ali Rifat and His wife Sister Yildiz at-Turki, Sheikh Dr. Omar of Maryland al-Hindi, Sheikh Tamer of Buffalo, and Sheikh Ali of Hartford Seminary, Sisters Asya Hamad, Amina Osman, and Fatima Samrodia of Darul-Ulum Madania of Buffalo for all their editing, suggestions and comments.

I want to also thank the team of Medina House Publishing in all their preparations and efforts at all stages of this book especially Br. Murat, Br. Khalid (Halit), Br. Mehmet (Matt) and Sister Karen.

Lastly, I would like to thank all of my family members for their patience with me during the preparation of this book.

We ask Allah ﷻ to accept all our efforts with the Divine Karam, Fadl, and Grace but not with our faulty and limited efforts deeming rejection. اللَّهُمَّ صلِّ عَلى سَيِّدِناَ وَ حَبِيْبِنَا وَ مَوْلَانَا مُحَمَّد.

INDEX

www.ingramcontent.com/pod-product-compliance
Lightning Source LLC
Chambersburg PA
CBHW032054090426
42744CB00005B/217

9 7 8 1 9 5 0 9 7 9 4 8 6